CYBERSECURITY
STUDY GUIDE

Mastering Cyber Security Defense to Shield Against

Identity Theft, Data breaches, Hackers, and more in

the Modern Age

|

Learn to Shield Against Identity Theft, data breaches,
Phishing, Ransomware, Hackers, and Beyond

Sam O.A

of the information contained herein, either explicitly or implicitly.

All copyrights not held by the publisher are owned by the respective author(s).

The information contained herein is provided solely for informational purposes and is therefore universal. The information is presented without contract or assurance of any kind.

The trademarks are used without the trademark owner's consent, and the trademark is published without the trademark owner's permission or support. All trademarks and brands mentioned in this book are solely for clarity purposes and are owned by their respective owners, who are not affiliated with this document.

For Questions and enquiries contact;

sam@samamoo.com

SA Publishing

SPECIAL BONUS!

Want These 2 Bonus EBooks For Free?

Get FREE, Unlimited Access To These and All of Our New Books By Joining Our Community

CLICK HERE TO JOIN

Other Books

- How to be More in Tune with The Feelings of Your Customers
- Time Management For Busy People

- Sell Like titans

Table of Contents

Introduction

In today's increasingly digital world, cybersecurity has become a pressing concern for individuals and organizations alike. With the rise of cyber threats such as *hacking, data breaches, and identity theft*, it is more important than ever to protect ourselves and our information from malicious actors. The **"Cybersecurity Study Guide: Mastering Cyber Security Defense to Shield Against Identity Theft, Data breaches, Hackers, and more in the Modern Age"**, provides a comprehensive guide to staying safe and secure in the digital age.

The book offers practical advice and insights on how to protect your personal and business information from cyber threats. This book covers a wide range of topics, including password management, email security, social engineering, and cloud security. The book also addresses the increasing threat of ransomware, phishing, and other forms of cybercrime, providing guidance on how to identify and prevent these attacks.

One of the key themes of the book is the importance of taking a proactive approach to cybersecurity. Sam emphasizes the need to stay vigilant and informed about the latest cyber threats and trends, and provides practical tips on how to stay up-to-date and protect yourself from these threats. The book also highlights the importance of developing a cybersecurity strategy that is tailored to your specific needs and risks.

Another important aspect of the book is its focus on the human element of cybersecurity. Sam recognizes that technology alone cannot provide complete protection against cyber threats, and emphasizes the importance of training and education in cybersecurity. This book provides guidance on how to educate yourself and your employees on best practices for staying safe online, and how to foster a culture of cybersecurity within your organization.

The book also addresses the growing concern of privacy in the digital age. Sam provides insights on how to protect your personal information online, including tips on social media privacy settings, encryption, and secure communication tools. He also discusses the role of government and corporations in protecting our privacy, and provides guidance on how to advocate for stronger privacy protections.

Sam uses case studies and real-world examples through out book to highlight the significance of cybersecurity and the repercussions of not taking it seriously. Additionally, he offers helpful tools and resources, such as suggested software and web sources, for readers to use in their own cybersecurity initiatives.

For anyone trying to keep secure and safe in the digital age, this book is a must-read. A thorough and useful guide to cybersecurity is provided in the book, along with information on current trends and dangers. The ideas provided by this book are more current and valuable than ever given the ongoing development of technology.

This book has something to offer everyone, whether you are a business leader trying to safeguard your organization's data, an individual worried about your own privacy and security, or a computer enthusiast trying to keep up with the newest cybersecurity developments. Anyone interested in cybersecurity and the potential it has to safeguard us and our information in the digital era should read this book because of Sam's lucid writing style and depth of knowledge and experience.

C h a p t e r   1

Practical Advice and Insights on Cybersecurity

Password Management

Password management is a critical aspect of cybersecurity in the modern world. As we rely more on digital services and platforms, maintaining strong and unique passwords becomes increasingly important to protect our personal and sensitive information from unauthorized access. In this comprehensive overview, we'll delve into the *significance of password management, best practices, and tools that can help enhance your digital security.*

Why is Password Management Important?

In the digital landscape, passwords serve as the first line of defense against unauthorized access to our online accounts and sensitive information. Effective password management is crucial because:

1. **Preventing unauthorized access:** Strong passwords make it significantly harder for hackers

to guess or crack them, reducing the risk of unauthorized access to your accounts.

2. **Protecting sensitive data:** Passwords are used to safeguard a wide range of sensitive information, including personal emails, financial accounts, social media profiles, and more. By managing your passwords effectively, you reduce the risk of identity theft, financial fraud, and other cybersecurity incidents.

3. **Combating password reuse:** Many people tend to reuse passwords across multiple accounts, making them vulnerable. If a hacker gains access to one account, they can potentially compromise all other accounts that share the same password. Effective password management encourages the use of unique passwords for each account, minimizing the impact of a security breach.

Best Practices for Password Management

To ensure robust password management, consider implementing the following best practices:

1. **Use complex and unique passwords:** Create

strong passwords that combine uppercase and lowercase letters, numbers, and special characters. Avoid using predictable phrases, easily guessable information (such as your name or birthdate), and common dictionary words. Additionally, use different passwords for each account to minimize the risk of widespread compromise.

2. **Enable multi-factor authentication (MFA):** Multi-factor authentication adds an extra layer of security by requiring users to provide additional verification, such as a fingerprint, a one-time password, or a security token, in addition to their password. Enable MFA whenever possible to strengthen your account security.

3. **Avoid sharing or writing down passwords:** Resist the temptation to share passwords with others or write them down on easily accessible mediums. If necessary, use reputable password management tools that offer secure password sharing features.

4. **Regularly update passwords:** It's essential to update your passwords periodically, ideally every few months or whenever there is a potential security breach or suspicion of compromise. Regularly

changing passwords reduces the risk of unauthorized access and ensures your accounts remain secure.

5. **Utilize password managers:** Password managers are convenient tools that securely store and manage your passwords. They typically encrypt your passwords with a master password or biometric authentication, making it easier to generate and store unique and complex passwords for different accounts. Password managers can also automatically fill in login information, simplifying the process of accessing your accounts securely.

Password Management Tools

Several password management tools are available to assist with effective password management. Here are a few popular examples:

1. **LastPass:** LastPass is a widely used password manager that securely stores passwords, generates strong ones, and synchronizes them across various devices.

2. **Dashlane:** Dashlane offers password management

features along with additional features like secure storage for personal data, form autofill, and a digital wallet.

3. **KeePass:** KeePass is an open-source password manager that allows you to store passwords in an encrypted database. It also supports generating strong passwords and has various plugins available for added functionality.

4. **1Password:** 1Password provides secure password storage, password generation, and sharing capabilities, along with the ability to store other sensitive data like credit card information and secure notes.

5. **Bitwarden:** Bitwarden is an open-source password manager that offers password storage, generation, and synchronization across multiple devices.

These password management tools provide a secure and convenient way to implement the best practices mentioned above, and offer additional features to enhance your password management experience. Some of these tools offer browser extensions, mobile apps, and cloud synchronization, allowing you to access your passwords securely from various devices.

When using a password manager, it's important to choose a reputable and trusted provider, as they will be responsible for securely storing your passwords. Look for features like strong encryption, zero-knowledge architecture (where the provider has no access to your passwords), and regular software updates to ensure the highest level of security.

Remember that while password managers can simplify the process of managing and securing your passwords, it's crucial to maintain the security of your master password or any authentication method used to access your password manager. Use a strong and unique master password, enable additional security measures like biometric authentication when available, and avoid sharing or storing your master password in an insecure manner.

In addition to utilizing password managers, it's important to stay informed about emerging security threats and follow recommended security practices. Be cautious of phishing attempts, regularly update your devices and software with the latest security patches, and exercise caution when accessing your accounts on public *Wi-Fi* networks.

By implementing effective password management practices, leveraging password management tools, and staying vigilant, you can significantly enhance your digital security and protect yourself from the increasing cybersecurity risks in the modern world.

Cybersecurity is an ongoing effort, and regularly reviewing and updating your password management approach is essential to stay ahead of evolving threats and ensure the safety of your digital presence.

1. **Password Complexity:** When creating passwords, it's important to focus on complexity. A strong password typically consists of a combination of uppercase and lowercase letters, numbers, and special characters. Avoid using easily guessable information such as names, birthdays, or common phrases. The longer and more diverse your password, the more resilient it is against brute-force attacks.

2. **Two-Factor Authentication (2FA):** Alongside strong passwords, enabling **2FA** adds an extra layer of security to your accounts. This method requires a second form of verification, such as a code sent to

your mobile device or a biometric scan, in addition to your password. Even if someone manages to obtain your password, they would still need the secondary authentication factor to gain access to your account.

3. **Password Rotation:** Regularly updating your passwords is a recommended practice to mitigate the impact of a potential security breach. Change passwords at least every three to six months, or immediately if there's a suspicion of compromise. Avoid reusing old passwords, and ensure the new ones follow the same principles of complexity and uniqueness.

4. **Phishing Awareness:** Phishing attacks are common methods used by hackers to trick individuals into revealing their passwords. Be cautious of suspicious emails, messages, or websites that ask for your login credentials. Always verify the legitimacy of the source before providing any sensitive information.

5. **Secure Password Storage:** When using a password manager, it's important to choose a trusted provider that prioritizes security. Look for features like end-

to-end encryption, strong access controls, and regular audits. Additionally, consider using a password manager that offers local encryption, where the encryption and decryption processes occur on your device rather than on the provider's servers.

6. **Security Hygiene:** Password management is just one part of overall security hygiene. It's crucial to maintain up-to-date antivirus software, regularly update your operating system and applications, and be cautious when downloading files or clicking on links from untrusted sources. These practices collectively contribute to a more robust security posture.

7. **Employee Education:** In corporate settings, organizations should prioritize employee education and awareness regarding password management. Conduct regular training sessions to promote best practices, emphasize the importance of strong passwords, and provide guidance on recognizing and reporting potential security threats.

Remember, while password management is a crucial aspect of cybersecurity, it's essential to adopt a holistic approach that encompasses various security measures to safeguard your digital presence effectively.

Email Security

Email security is of paramount importance in today's digital world, where email remains a primary communication channel for individuals and businesses alike. Safeguarding email accounts and protecting sensitive information transmitted through email is critical to prevent unauthorized access, data breaches, and phishing attacks. In this extensive overview, we'll delve into the significance of email security, common threats and vulnerabilities, and best practices to enhance email security.

The Significance of Email Security

Email serves as a common platform for exchanging personal, financial, and confidential information. Effective email security measures are crucial for several reasons:

1. **Data Protection:** Emails often contain sensitive

data such as financial details, personal information, trade secrets, or intellectual property. Ensuring the security of this data is essential to maintain privacy, comply with regulations (such as GDPR or HIPAA), and prevent unauthorized access or data leaks.

2. **Phishing and Social Engineering:** Email is frequently exploited by cybercriminals to launch phishing attacks, where they trick recipients into disclosing sensitive information or clicking on malicious links or attachments. Strong email security helps detect and block these fraudulent attempts, minimizing the risk of falling victim to scams or identity theft.

3. **Malware and Ransomware:** Email is a common vector for delivering malware and ransomware to unsuspecting users. Opening an infected email attachment or clicking on a malicious link can lead to malware infections or even the encryption of critical data. Robust email security measures help detect and block such threats, mitigating the risk of compromising systems and data.

Common Threats and Vulnerabilities in Email Security

To effectively secure email accounts, it's crucial to understand the common threats and vulnerabilities associated with email:

1. **Phishing:** Phishing emails often masquerade as legitimate messages from trusted sources, aiming to deceive recipients into revealing sensitive information, such as passwords or financial details. They may also lead users to malicious websites or prompt them to download malware-infected attachments.

2. **Email Spoofing:** Email spoofing involves forging the sender's email address to make it appear as if the email originates from a trusted source. This technique is frequently used in phishing attacks to trick recipients into believing the email is legitimate.

3. **Man-in-the-Middle Attacks:** In these attacks, cybercriminals intercept email communications between the sender and recipient, allowing them to eavesdrop, alter the content, or steal sensitive

information exchanged via email.

4. **Malware and Ransomware:** Email attachments or links can deliver malicious software that can compromise the security and integrity of systems and data. Malware can include viruses, worms, trojans, spyware, or ransomware that encrypts files and demands a ransom for their release.

Best Practices for Email Security

Implementing robust email security practices can significantly enhance protection against email-related threats. Consider the following best practices:

1. **Strong Passwords:** Use unique and complex passwords for your email accounts. Include a mix of uppercase and lowercase letters, numbers, and special characters. Avoid using easily guessable information and enable *multi-factor authentication (MFA)* whenever possible for an additional layer of security.

2. **Strong Passwords:** Use strong, unique passwords for each email account, consisting of a mix of letters, numbers, and symbols. Avoid using

common words or personal information that can be easily guessed. Use a password manager to generate and store complex passwords securely.

3. **Anti-Malware and Anti-Spam Protection:** Utilize reliable anti-malware and anti-spam software to detect and filter out potentially malicious emails and attachments. These tools can help identify and block phishing attempts, suspicious links, and malware-infected content.

4. **Encryption:** Consider using email encryption technologies, such as *Secure Sockets Layer (SSL) or Transport Layer Security (TLS),* to encrypt the communication between email servers and clients. Encryption ensures that the contents of your emails remain secure and inaccessible to unauthorized individuals.

5. **Email Filters and Firewalls:** Enable email filters and firewalls to block suspicious or malicious content. These mechanisms can automatically detect and quarantine emails with known spam patterns, malware signatures, or malicious attachments.

5. **Secure Authentication Protocols:** Ensure that

your email provider supports secure authentication protocols such as *Secure Sockets Layer/Transport Layer Security (SSL/TLS)* and *Internet Message Access Protocol (IMAP)* over **SSL/TLS**. These protocols encrypt the communication between email clients and servers, protecting the confidentiality of the data transmitted.

6. **Be Cautious of Phishing Attempts:** Exercise caution when opening emails, especially those from unknown or suspicious senders. Avoid clicking on links or downloading attachments from untrusted sources. Verify the legitimacy of emails, particularly those requesting sensitive information or urging urgent action, by contacting the supposed sender through a separate channel.

7. **Regular Software Updates:** Keep your email client, operating system, and security software up to date. Software updates often include security patches that address vulnerabilities and protect against newly identified threats.

8. **User Education and Awareness:** Educate yourself and your employees about email security best practices. Promote awareness of common email

threats, such as phishing and social engineering, and provide guidance on how to identify and report suspicious emails. Regularly remind users to exercise caution and not to disclose sensitive information via email unless verified through secure means.

9. **Secure Network Connections:** When accessing your email account, ensure that you're using a secure and trusted network connection. Avoid using public **Wi-Fi** networks, as they can be susceptible to eavesdropping and man-in-the-middle attacks. If necessary, use a *virtual private network (VPN)* to encrypt your internet traffic and ensure secure communication.

10. **Regular Backups:** Regularly backup your important email data to a secure location. In case of data loss or a ransomware attack, having backups ensures that you can restore your emails and recover any lost information.

11. **Email Security Policies:** Establish email security policies within organizations to define acceptable use, password requirements, encryption practices, and reporting procedures for suspicious emails.

Regularly review and update these policies to align with emerging threats and best practices.

12. **Ongoing Monitoring and Incident Response:** Implement mechanisms to monitor email traffic for abnormalities or signs of compromise. Set up alerts and notifications for potential security incidents and establish an incident response plan to mitigate and address any breaches or security issues promptly.

By adopting these best practices and implementing robust email security measures, individuals and organizations can significantly enhance their protection against email-based threats, reduce the risk of data breaches, and safeguard sensitive information.

Email security requires a multi-layered approach, combining technical controls, user awareness, and proactive monitoring to stay ahead of evolving threats and protect against unauthorized access or data loss.

Social Engineering

Certainly! *Social engineering* is a technique used by malicious individuals to manipulate and deceive people into divulging sensitive information, performing certain actions, or providing unauthorized access to secure systems. It exploits human psychology and trust to bypass traditional security measures. In the context of cybersecurity and digital survival, understanding social engineering is crucial as it remains one of the most prevalent and effective tactics used by attackers to gain unauthorized access to personal and confidential information.

Social engineering attacks can take various forms and can occur through different channels, such as email, phone calls, instant messaging, or even in-person interactions. Attackers leverage psychological tactics to manipulate human behavior, exploit trust, and exploit vulnerabilities in individuals and organizations.

Here are some common social engineering techniques:

1. **Phishing:** Phishing is a widespread social engineering technique where attackers send fraudulent emails that appear to be from legitimate sources, such as banks, social media platforms, or trusted organizations. These emails often contain urgent requests for personal information or prompt recipients to click on malicious links or download

infected attachments.

2. **Pretexting:** Pretexting involves creating a fictional scenario or pretext to trick individuals into revealing sensitive information. Attackers may impersonate someone in authority, such as a company executive or IT support personnel, and use this guise to manipulate victims into providing access credentials or confidential data.

3. **Baiting:** Baiting involves offering something enticing or appealing to individuals in exchange for their sensitive information or access to systems. Attackers may use physical media like infected *USB drives* or create fake websites or downloads to entice victims to enter their credentials or disclose personal data.

4. **Tailgating:** Tailgating refers to the act of following someone who has authorized access to a secured area without proper authentication. Attackers may exploit a person's natural inclination to hold the door open for others or pretend to be an employee or contractor to gain physical access to restricted areas.

5. **Impersonation:** Impersonation occurs when

attackers pose as someone else to deceive individuals and gain their trust. This can involve impersonating a colleague, a technical support representative, or a service provider to trick victims into providing sensitive information or granting access to systems.

Protecting against social engineering attacks requires a combination of technical measures and user awareness. Here are some key strategies to defend against social engineering:

1. **Education and Awareness:** Train individuals to recognize social engineering techniques, understand the risks, and be cautious when sharing sensitive information or responding to unsolicited requests. Regularly educate employees about the latest social engineering tactics and provide real-world examples to enhance their awareness.

2. **Verify Requests:** Always verify requests for sensitive information or actions before complying. Contact the supposed sender or requester directly through a known and trusted communication channel to confirm the legitimacy of the request.

3. **Strong Authentication:** Implement strong authentication measures such as multi-factor authentication (MFA) to add an extra layer of security. This reduces the risk of unauthorized access even if an attacker manages to obtain some login credentials through social engineering.

4. **Implement Email Filters and Anti-Malware Software:** Deploy robust email filters and anti-malware software to detect and block phishing emails, suspicious attachments, or links. These security measures can help prevent malicious emails from reaching users' inboxes.

5. **Physical Security Measures:** Implement physical security controls to restrict unauthorized access to sensitive areas. This can include the use of access cards, security personnel, surveillance cameras, and visitor management systems to deter social engineering attempts.

6. **Incident Response and Reporting:** Establish clear incident response procedures to handle and report social engineering incidents promptly. Encourage employees to report any suspicious activities or potential social engineering attempts to the

appropriate security team.

7. **Regular Updates and Patching:** Keep software, operating systems, and applications up to date with the latest security patches. Vulnerabilities in software can be exploited by social engineers, so regular updates and patching help mitigate those risks.

8. **Limit Information Exposure:** Be mindful of the information shared online, especially on social media platforms. Attackers often gather personal details from social media profiles to tailor their social engineering attacks. Minimize the amount of personal information available publicly and adjust privacy settings to restrict access to sensitive information.

9. **Implement Security Policies:** Establish and enforce security policies that outline best practices for handling sensitive information, responding to requests for data, and interacting with unfamiliar individuals or organizations. Regularly communicate and reinforce these policies to employees.

10. **Conduct Security Awareness Training:**

Regularly conduct security awareness training programs to educate employees about social engineering tactics, warning signs, and proper response procedures. Training sessions can simulate real-world scenarios and provide employees with hands-on experience in identifying and responding to social engineering attacks.

11. **Encourage a Culture of Security:** Foster a security-conscious culture within the organization where employees are encouraged to be vigilant, question suspicious requests, and report potential security incidents. Promote an environment where employees feel comfortable seeking guidance or clarification when faced with uncertain situations.

12. **Regular Security Assessments:** Conduct regular security assessments, including penetration testing and social engineering simulations, to identify vulnerabilities and areas for improvement. These assessments help uncover weaknesses in security controls and provide insights for strengthening defenses against social engineering attacks.

Remember, social engineering attacks exploit human psychology and vulnerabilities, making user awareness and education critical.

By combining technical measures, employee training, and a proactive security approach, organizations can significantly reduce the risk of falling victim to social engineering attacks and protect their sensitive information.

Cloud Security

Cloud security refers to the practices and technologies implemented to protect data, applications, and infrastructure in cloud computing environments. It encompasses a range of security measures and controls designed to ensure confidentiality, integrity, and availability of data stored, processed, and transmitted in the cloud.

History of Cloud Computing

Cloud computing has evolved rapidly over the years, and as its adoption has grown, so has the importance of cloud security. The concept of cloud computing emerged in the 1960s with the development of time-sharing systems. However, it gained widespread recognition and popularity with the advent of virtualization and the Internet in the early 2000s. As businesses and individuals started leveraging cloud services for storage, computing power, and software applications, the need for robust security measures to protect sensitive information became evident.

Uses of Cloud Computing

Cloud security is relevant to various cloud deployment models, including *public, private, and hybrid clouds*. It applies to *Infrastructure as a Service (IaaS)*, *Platform as a Service (PaaS)*, and *Software as a Service (SaaS)* offerings.

Cloud security measures are employed to safeguard data and applications hosted in the cloud, secure network connections between cloud environments and end-users, and protect cloud infrastructure from unauthorized access and attacks.

Importance of Cloud Computing

Cloud security is essential for several reasons:

1. **Data Protection:** Cloud security ensures that sensitive data stored in the cloud remains

confidential and protected against unauthorized access. It involves encryption, access controls, and data loss prevention measures.

2. **Compliance and Legal Requirements:** Many industries have strict regulatory requirements regarding the protection of data, such as **HIPAA** for healthcare or **GDPR** for personal data. Cloud security helps organizations meet these compliance obligations and mitigate legal risks.

3. **Business Continuity:** Cloud security includes backup and disaster recovery measures that help ensure business continuity in case of data loss, natural disasters, or other disruptive events. Redundancy, data replication, and failover mechanisms are essential components.

4. **Scalability and Flexibility:** Cloud security enables businesses to scale their infrastructure and resources as needed while maintaining the necessary security controls. It allows organizations to adapt quickly to changing business requirements without compromising security.

5. **Shared Responsibility Model:** Cloud security requires a clear understanding of the shared

responsibility model between cloud service providers and cloud users. While cloud providers are responsible for securing the underlying infrastructure, users are responsible for securing their data, applications, and user access.

Disadvantages of Cloud Computing

While cloud computing offers numerous benefits, there are potential disadvantages related to cloud security:

1. **Data Breaches:** Cloud environments can be targeted by attackers, and if security measures are not implemented effectively, data breaches can occur. Unauthorized access to sensitive information can result in financial loss, reputational damage, and legal repercussions.

2. **Dependency on Service Providers:** Organizations relying on cloud services have a level of dependency on cloud service providers. If the provider experiences a security incident or fails to meet service-level agreements, it can impact the security and availability of the organization's data and applications.

3. **Insider Threats:** Cloud security also encompasses addressing insider threats, which involve malicious activities by individuals with authorized access to the cloud environment. Organizations need to implement proper access controls, monitoring, and employee training to mitigate these risks.

4. **Limited Control:** Organizations may have limited control over the security measures implemented by cloud service providers. They must thoroughly assess the provider's security capabilities, certifications, and compliance with relevant standards to ensure the security of their data.

It's important to note that while cloud security introduces unique challenges, many of these concerns can be effectively addressed through proper planning, risk assessment, security controls, and adherence to best practices.

Here is some additional information on cloud security:

1. **Security Controls:** Cloud security encompasses a range of controls and mechanisms to protect cloud environments. These include identity and access management (IAM), encryption, network security,

intrusion detection and prevention systems (IDPS), firewalls, vulnerability scanning, and security information and event management (SIEM) systems.

2. **Multi-tenancy:** In a public cloud environment, multiple organizations or users share the same underlying infrastructure. Proper isolation and segregation of data and resources are crucial to prevent unauthorized access or data leakage between tenants.

3. **Cloud Service Level Agreements (SLAs):** Cloud service providers typically offer SLAs that define the level of security, availability, and reliability they guarantee. It is important for organizations to review and understand these SLAs to ensure they align with their security requirements and risk tolerance.

4. **Cloud Security Standards and Certifications:** Various cloud security standards and certifications exist to assess the security practices of cloud service providers. Examples include *ISO 27001, CSA STAR Certification, FedRAMP, and SOC 2.* Evaluating a provider's compliance with these standards can help

determine their commitment to security.

5. **Cloud Security Assessments:** Conducting regular security assessments, such as vulnerability scanning, penetration testing, and security audits, helps identify vulnerabilities and weaknesses in cloud environments. These assessments should be performed both by the cloud service provider and the cloud user to ensure comprehensive security coverage.

6. **Continuous Monitoring and Incident Response:** Implementing robust monitoring solutions allows organizations to detect and respond to security incidents promptly. Cloud environments should be monitored for suspicious activities, unauthorized access attempts, and other indicators of compromise. Incident response plans and procedures should be established to address security breaches effectively.

7. **Data Residency and Compliance:** Organizations operating in certain jurisdictions or industries may have legal or regulatory requirements regarding data residency and privacy. Cloud security should address these requirements, ensuring that data is

stored and processed in compliance with applicable laws and regulations.

8. **Third-Party Risk Management:** Cloud environments often involve the integration of third-party services or components. It is crucial to assess the security posture of these third parties and ensure they have appropriate security measures in place. This includes conducting due diligence, reviewing their security practices, and implementing contractual agreements to protect data and mitigate risks.

9. **Cloud Security Training and Awareness:** Organizations should provide training and awareness programs for employees and stakeholders to educate them about cloud security risks, best practices, and their roles and responsibilities in maintaining secure cloud environments.

10. **Security Incident Response and Forensics:** In the event of a security incident or breach, cloud environments should have well-defined incident response and forensic investigation processes in place. This includes preserving evidence,

conducting forensic analysis, and implementing corrective measures to prevent future incidents.

Cloud security is a complex and evolving field. It requires a combination of technical controls, risk management practices, and ongoing vigilance to ensure the integrity, confidentiality, and availability of data and services in cloud environments.

Prevention of Ransomware, Phishing, and Other Forms of Cybercrime

Here's an extensive overview of prevention strategies for ransomware, phishing, and other forms of cybercrime:

1. **Ransomware Prevention:**
   - **Regular Data Backup:** Implement a robust backup strategy to ensure critical data is regularly backed up and stored offline or in an isolated network. This helps mitigate the impact of ransomware attacks by allowing data restoration without paying the ransom.
   - **Security Software:** Deploy reputable antivirus and anti-malware solutions that provide real-time protection against ransomware. Keep security software up to date to defend against the latest threats.
   - **Software Patching:** Keep operating systems, applications, and software up to date with the latest security patches and updates. Vulnerabilities in software can be exploited by ransomware attacks, so timely patching is

crucial.

- **User Awareness:** Educate employees and users about ransomware threats, warning signs, and safe computing practices. Train them to be cautious of suspicious emails, links, and downloads.

- **Email and Web Filtering:** Implement robust email and web filtering solutions that can detect and block malicious content, attachments, and phishing attempts.

- **Restrict Privileges:** Limit user privileges to prevent unauthorized access and the spread of ransomware within the network. Users should only have access to the resources necessary for their roles.

- **Network Segmentation:** Implement network segmentation to isolate critical systems and data from the rest of the network. This helps contain the spread of ransomware and limits its impact.

2. **Phishing Prevention:**

- **User Education:** Conduct regular security awareness training to educate employees and users about phishing techniques, how to identify suspicious emails, and how to respond appropriately.

- **Strong Authentication:** Encourage the use of strong, unique passwords and implement multi-factor authentication (MFA) to add an extra layer of protection against phishing attacks.

- **Email Filtering:** Utilize email filtering solutions that can detect and block phishing emails, spam, and malicious attachments. These filters can help prevent phishing emails from reaching users' inboxes.

- **URL Inspection:** Implement URL inspection mechanisms to verify the reputation and safety of website links. Users should be cautious when clicking on links in emails or other communications.

- **Reporting Mechanisms:** Establish a clear reporting process for users to report suspicious emails or potential phishing attempts. Prompt reporting allows for swift action and incident response.

- **Security Updates:** Keep software, web browsers, and plugins up to date with the latest security patches. Vulnerabilities in software can be exploited by phishing attacks, so timely patching is crucial.

3. **General Cybercrime Prevention:**

    - **Strong Passwords:** Encourage the use of strong and unique passwords for all accounts. Consider implementing password managers to help users generate and securely store complex passwords.

    - **User Access Control:** Implement the principle of least privilege, ensuring that users have the minimum required access rights to perform their tasks. Regularly review and revoke unnecessary privileges.

    - **Network Security:** Deploy firewalls, intrusion detection and prevention systems (IDPS), and network segmentation to protect against unauthorized access and attacks.

    - **Regular Security Updates:** Keep all software and systems up to date with the latest security patches and updates. This includes operating systems, applications, firmware, and network equipment.

- **Data Encryption:** Utilize encryption techniques to protect sensitive data, both in transit and at rest. Encryption adds an extra layer of security and helps prevent unauthorized access.

- **Incident Response Planning:** Develop a comprehensive incident response plan that outlines the steps to be taken in case of a cybercrime incident. This includes communication channels, reporting mechanisms, and recovery procedures.

- **Employee Training and Awareness:** Continuously educate employees and users about common cybercrime techniques, best practices for data protection, safe browsing habits, and the importance of reporting suspicious activities.

It's important to note that prevention measures should be implemented continuously and regularly reviewed to adapt to emerging threats and changing cybersecurity landscape. Organizations should also consider the following additional prevention strategies:

4. **Security Assessments:** Conduct regular security assessments, such as penetration testing and vulnerability scanning, to identify weaknesses and vulnerabilities in systems and applications. Address any identified issues promptly to mitigate potential risks.

5. **Secure Configuration Management:** Follow secure configuration guidelines for all systems, applications, and devices. Disable unnecessary services, remove default accounts and passwords, and apply appropriate security configurations to minimize the attack surface.

6. **Incident Monitoring and Detection:** Implement security monitoring solutions, such as *Security Information and Event Management (SIEM)* systems and intrusion detection systems (IDS), to detect and respond to cyber threats in real-time. Monitor network traffic, system logs, and user activity for signs of compromise.

7. **Security Patches and Updates:** Keep all software, including operating systems, applications, and firmware, up to date with the latest security patches

and updates. Implement a robust patch management process to ensure timely deployment of patches.

8. **Web Application Security:** Implement secure coding practices and conduct regular security testing of web applications to identify and address vulnerabilities. Utilize *web application firewalls (WAFs)* to protect against common web-based attacks.

9. **Endpoint Protection:** Deploy endpoint protection solutions, such as *endpoint security software* and *host intrusion prevention systems (HIPS)*, to protect individual devices from malware, unauthorized access, and data breaches.

10. **Data Loss Prevention (DLP):** Implement DLP solutions to monitor and control the flow of sensitive data within and outside the organization. DLP tools can help prevent accidental or malicious data leaks by enforcing data protection policies.

11. **Regular Security Awareness Training:** Continuously educate employees and users about the latest cybersecurity threats and attack techniques. Train them to recognize social engineering attempts, suspicious behavior, and to

report potential security incidents.

12. **Incident Response Readiness:** Develop an incident response plan that outlines the steps to be taken in case of a cybersecurity incident. This includes establishing a designated incident response team, defining communication channels, and conducting regular drills and simulations.

It's important to note that no prevention strategy is foolproof, and organizations should also invest in robust incident response and recovery capabilities. Cybersecurity is an ongoing process that requires a combination of preventive measures, user education, technological solutions, and timely incident response to mitigate the risks associated with cybercrime.

Summary

This chapter provides a comprehensive overview of various aspects of cybersecurity, emphasizing the importance of staying informed and vigilant. It covers the evolving cyber threat landscape, the consequences of negligence, strategies for achieving awareness, and the role of individuals and organizations in building a resilient cybersecurity culture. The book highlights the significance of staying updated on emerging threats, understanding security best practices, and cultivating a proactive mindset. It also explores the importance of information sharing, engaging with experts, implementing security awareness programs, and fostering collaboration across departments. By following the practical advice and insights provided in this book, individuals and organizations can enhance their cybersecurity posture and better protect themselves against cyber threats.

Action Points

1. **Stay Informed:** Regularly seek updated information on emerging cyber threats, attack techniques, and security best practices. Follow reputable security news sources, industry reports, and engage with cybersecurity communities to stay abreast of the latest developments.

2. **Implement Security Best Practices:** Adopt robust security practices such as using strong and unique passwords, keeping software and systems up to date with the latest patches, encrypting sensitive data, and implementing multi-factor authentication

(MFA) where possible.

3. **Engage with Experts:** Seek guidance from cybersecurity experts, consultants, and *managed security service providers (MSSPs)* to assess your organization's security posture, identify vulnerabilities, and implement effective security measures tailored to your specific needs.

4. **Establish a Security Awareness Program:** Develop and implement a comprehensive security awareness program within your organization. Provide regular training sessions, simulate phishing exercises, and reinforce security-conscious behaviors through internal communications and recognition programs.

5. **Foster Collaboration and Accountability:** Promote a culture of cybersecurity collaboration across departments and encourage employees to take ownership of their cybersecurity responsibilities. Establish clear reporting channels for security incidents and continuously evaluate and improve your security measures based on lessons learned.

Chapter 2

Proactive Approach to Cybersecurity

The Importance of Staying Informed and Vigilant

In today's digital age, where technology permeates every aspect of our lives, staying informed and vigilant about cybersecurity threats has become paramount. The rapid evolution of technology has opened new doors of convenience, connectivity, and productivity. However, it has also introduced a complex web of cybersecurity challenges, where malicious actors exploit vulnerabilities for their gain. In this ever-changing landscape, individuals and organizations must recognize the critical importance of staying informed and vigilant to safeguard their digital assets and privacy.

This comprehensive book explores the reasons why staying informed and vigilant is crucial, the potential consequences of negligence, effective strategies for achieving awareness, and the role of individuals and organizations in building a resilient cybersecurity culture.

Understanding the Cybersecurity Landscape

A. Evolution of Cyber Threats: This section delves into the dynamic nature of cybersecurity threats, including the rise of sophisticated attacks such as ransomware, phishing, social engineering, and advanced persistent threats. It highlights the motivation of threat actors and the shifting tactics they employ to exploit vulnerabilities in technology and human behavior.

B. Increasing Cybersecurity Risks: The interconnectedness of devices, systems, and networks has amplified the potential impact of cyber threats. This subsection discusses the expanding attack surface, emphasizing the vulnerabilities posed by the Internet of Things (IoT), cloud computing, mobile devices, and social media.

C. Real-World Consequences: Drawing from prominent cyber incidents and data breaches, this section outlines the tangible repercussions of cybersecurity breaches. It examines the financial, reputational, and legal consequences faced by individuals, businesses, and even nations, underscoring the urgency of proactive cybersecurity measures.

The Importance of Staying Informed

A. Awareness of Emerging Threats: Highlighting the rapidly evolving nature of cybersecurity threats, this section emphasizes the need to stay informed about new attack vectors, tactics, and vulnerabilities. It explores the role of threat intelligence, security news sources, and industry reports in acquiring up-to-date knowledge.

B. Recognizing Social Engineering Techniques: Social engineering attacks, such as phishing, vishing, and smishing, prey on human psychology and trust. This subsection underscores the significance of staying informed about social engineering tactics to effectively identify and thwart such attacks.

C. Understanding Security Best Practices: Staying informed about security best practices enables individuals and organizations to adopt robust preventive measures. It covers topics such as password management, secure browsing habits, software patching, data encryption, and network security practices.

D. Privacy and Data Protection: The importance of staying informed about privacy regulations, data protection laws, and consumer rights is explored in this section. It highlights the significance of understanding data privacy policies, consent mechanisms, and the implications of sharing personal information.

The Role of Vigilance in Cybersecurity

A. Cultivating a Security Mindset: This section emphasizes the significance of developing a proactive and vigilant mindset towards cybersecurity. It explores the concept of the "human firewall" and discusses the role of individuals as the first line of defense in recognizing and reporting potential threats.

B. Security Hygiene: Maintaining good security hygiene through regular system updates, strong password practices, and safe online behaviors is crucial. This subsection provides practical tips for individuals to enhance their cybersecurity posture and remain vigilant.

C. Incident Reporting and Response: Highlighting the importance of promptly reporting security incidents, this section emphasizes the need for individuals and organizations to establish clear reporting channels and incident response procedures. It also emphasizes the role of cybersecurity incident response teams in managing and mitigating the impact of breaches.

D. Continuous Education and Training: This subsection emphasizes the need for continuous education and training in cybersecurity. It discusses the importance of staying updated with the latest trends, emerging threats, and evolving defense mechanisms. It highlights the role of cybersecurity certifications, workshops, webinars, and online resources in enhancing knowledge and skills.

Strategies for Achieving Awareness

A. Information Sharing and Collaboration: This section emphasizes the significance of information sharing and collaboration among individuals, organizations, and cybersecurity communities. It explores the role of threat intelligence sharing platforms, industry forums, and public-private partnerships in fostering a collective defense against cyber threats.

B. Engaging with Security Experts: Encouraging individuals and organizations to engage with cybersecurity experts, this subsection discusses the benefits of seeking professional advice, conducting security assessments, and partnering with *managed security service providers (MSSPs).*

C. Security Awareness Programs: Establishing security awareness programs within organizations is crucial. This section explores the key components of effective awareness programs, including training modules, simulated phishing exercises, and ongoing reinforcement through newsletters, posters, and internal communications.

D. Government Initiatives and Regulations: Governments play a vital role in promoting cybersecurity awareness and enforcing regulations. This subsection examines the role of government agencies, cybersecurity frameworks, and initiatives aimed at raising awareness and fostering a secure digital environment.

Building a Resilient Cybersecurity Culture

A. Leadership and Accountability: This section emphasizes the importance of leadership commitment to cybersecurity. It explores the role of executives and managers in setting the tone for cybersecurity practices, establishing policies, and allocating resources for security initiatives.

B. Employee Engagement: Engaging employees in cybersecurity efforts is essential for building a resilient cybersecurity culture. This subsection discusses the benefits of fostering a sense of responsibility, providing training and resources, and recognizing and rewarding security-conscious behaviors.

C. Collaboration across Departments: Effective cybersecurity requires collaboration across departments within an organization. This section highlights the importance of integrating cybersecurity into various business functions, including *IT, human resources, legal, and compliance.*

D. Continuous Improvement and Adaptability: Cybersecurity is an ongoing process. This subsection emphasizes the need for organizations to continuously evaluate their security posture, learn from incidents and security breaches, and adapt their strategies to address evolving threats.

Staying informed and vigilant in the face of cyber threats is not just an individual responsibility but a collective endeavor. This book has underscored the importance of staying informed about emerging threats, understanding security best practices, and recognizing the role of vigilance in maintaining cybersecurity. It has explored strategies for achieving awareness, including information sharing, engaging with experts, implementing security awareness programs, and government initiatives. Additionally, it has emphasized the significance of building a resilient cybersecurity culture through leadership commitment, employee engagement, departmental collaboration, and continuous improvement. By staying informed and remaining vigilant, individuals and organizations can better protect themselves against cybercrime, safeguard their digital assets, and contribute to a safer and more secure digital ecosystem.

Developing a Tailored Cybersecurity Strategy

In today's interconnected and digitized world, organizations face an ever-evolving landscape of cybersecurity threats. The increasing frequency and sophistication of cyber attacks make it imperative for businesses to develop a tailored cybersecurity strategy that addresses their unique needs and vulnerabilities. A one-size-fits-all approach is insufficient, as each organization possesses distinct assets, risks, and operational requirements. This comprehensive book delves into the process of developing a tailored cybersecurity strategy, covering key considerations, steps, and best practices. By following this guidance, organizations can strengthen their cybersecurity defenses, protect their valuable digital assets, and safeguard their reputation.

Assessing Your Cybersecurity Landscape

A. Identify Assets and Critical Information: Begin by conducting an inventory of your digital assets, including systems, networks, databases, intellectual property, customer data, and sensitive information. Determine their value and importance to your organization's operations.

B. Analyze Threats and Risks: Assess the potential threats and risks that your organization faces. This involves evaluating external threats (e.g., malware, phishing, ransomware) as well as internal risks (e.g., insider threats, unauthorized access). Consider the impact and likelihood of each risk scenario.

C. Compliance and Regulatory Requirements: Understand the legal and regulatory frameworks relevant to your industry. Identify compliance obligations and ensure your cybersecurity strategy aligns with these requirements, including data privacy regulations and industry-specific standards.

Defining Objectives and Goals

A. Establish Security Objectives: Based on the assessment, define clear and measurable cybersecurity objectives that align with your organizational goals. Examples include protecting customer data, maintaining operational continuity, and enhancing incident response capabilities.

B. Prioritize Risk Mitigation: Identify and prioritize the most critical risks based on their potential impact and likelihood. Develop a risk mitigation plan that outlines specific actions and controls to address each identified risk.

C. Involve Stakeholders: Engage stakeholders from different departments, including IT, legal, compliance, finance, and operations, to gain a comprehensive understanding of their requirements and concerns. Foster collaboration and ensure buy-in from key decision-makers.

Developing Security Policies and Procedures

A. Access Control and Authentication: Establish policies for user access management, including role-based access controls (RBAC), strong authentication mechanisms (e.g., multi-factor authentication), and regular review of user privileges.

B. Data Protection and Privacy: Implement policies and procedures for data classification, encryption, data handling, and data retention. Ensure compliance with applicable data protection regulations and adopt privacy-by-design principles.

C. Incident Response and Business Continuity: Develop a robust incident response plan that outlines roles, responsibilities, communication channels, and incident escalation procedures. Test the plan through simulations and regular drills. Additionally, establish a business continuity plan to ensure operational resilience in the event of a cyber incident.

D. Security Awareness and Training: Foster a culture of security awareness by providing regular training to employees on cybersecurity best practices, phishing awareness, password hygiene, and social engineering threats. Encourage reporting of security incidents and provide mechanisms for anonymous reporting.

Implementing Technical Controls

A. Network Security: Deploy firewalls, intrusion detection and prevention systems, and secure network segmentation to protect against unauthorized access and malicious activities. Regularly monitor network traffic and implement security updates.

B. Endpoint Protection: Implement endpoint security solutions, including *anti-malware software, host-based intrusion detection systems (HIDS),* and device encryption. Enforce security configurations and regularly patch endpoint devices.

C. Secure Software Development: Establish secure coding practices, perform code reviews, and conduct regular security assessments to identify and remediate vulnerabilities in your software applications. Implement secure development frameworks and practices, such as the *OWASP Top Ten*, to ensure the development of secure and resilient software.

D. Data Backup and Recovery: Regularly backup

critical data and ensure the backups are stored securely. Test data restoration processes to ensure data can be recovered effectively in case of a cyber incident or data loss event.

E. Continuous Monitoring and Threat Intelligence: Implement robust monitoring systems that provide real-time visibility into your network, systems, and applications. Leverage threat intelligence feeds and security information and event management (SIEM) tools to detect and respond to potential threats promptly.

Continuous Evaluation and Improvement

A. Regular Assessments and Audits: Conduct periodic cybersecurity assessments and audits to identify any gaps or weaknesses in your security measures. This includes vulnerability assessments, penetration testing, and compliance audits.

B. Incident Response Testing: Regularly test your incident response plan through tabletop exercises and simulated cyber incident scenarios. Identify areas for improvement and update the plan accordingly.

C. Security Awareness and Training: Continuously

educate and train employees on emerging threats, new attack techniques, and evolving best practices. Stay updated with the latest cybersecurity trends and provide relevant training materials and resources.

D. Collaboration and Information Sharing: Engage in collaborative efforts with industry peers, cybersecurity communities, and government agencies to share information and best practices. Participate in threat sharing platforms and forums to stay informed about the latest threats and mitigation strategies.

E. Stay Abreast of Regulatory Changes: Monitor regulatory developments and changes in cybersecurity requirements. Ensure ongoing compliance with applicable regulations and standards by conducting regular assessments and updating policies and procedures as needed.

Developing a tailored cybersecurity strategy is essential for organizations to effectively protect their digital assets and mitigate cyber risks. By conducting a thorough assessment of their cybersecurity landscape, defining clear objectives and goals, and implementing robust security policies, procedures, and technical controls, organizations can enhance their cybersecurity posture. Continuous evaluation, improvement, and collaboration with stakeholders and industry peers are crucial for maintaining an effective cybersecurity strategy in the face of evolving threats. With a proactive approach to cybersecurity, organizations can better safeguard their valuable assets, maintain trust with customers and partners, and navigate the digital landscape with confidence.

Training and Education in Cybersecurity

In the rapidly evolving world of cybersecurity, where threats are becoming more sophisticated and pervasive, organizations and individuals must prioritize training and education to stay ahead of cybercriminals. This comprehensive book explores the importance of training and education in cybersecurity, highlighting its role in equipping professionals with the knowledge, skills, and mindset needed to protect digital assets. It delves into various aspects of cybersecurity training and education, including professional certifications, academic programs, practical hands-on training, and ongoing learning opportunities. By investing in comprehensive training and education initiatives, organizations can build a skilled cybersecurity workforce and strengthen their defense against cyber threats.

The Significance of Cybersecurity Training:

In today's interconnected world, cyber threats pose significant risks to organizations of all sizes. Cybersecurity training plays a crucial role in preparing professionals to defend against these threats. It provides individuals with a solid foundation in cybersecurity concepts, principles, and best practices. By staying current with the latest trends and emerging threats, professionals can develop proactive strategies and implement effective security measures. Cybersecurity training offers several benefits:

A. Enhanced Skills and Knowledge: Comprehensive training programs equip individuals with the technical skills and knowledge required to identify, prevent, and respond to cyber threats. Training covers a wide range of topics, including network security, secure coding practices, incident response, and ethical hacking. By acquiring these skills, professionals can better protect organizations from cyber attacks and mitigate the potential damage.

B. Professional Certifications: Certifications in cybersecurity validate the expertise and knowledge of professionals in specific domains. Industry-recognized certifications, such as *Certified Information Systems Security Professional (CISSP), Certified Ethical Hacker (CEH), and Certified Information Security Manager (CISM)*, demonstrate a commitment to excellence and provide a competitive edge in the job market. Certifications also serve as a benchmark for employers when evaluating the skills and qualifications of potential hires.

C. Practical Hands-On Training: Practical, hands-on training exercises and simulations allow professionals to apply their knowledge in real-world scenarios. Cybersecurity training programs often include practical labs, simulated attacks, and vulnerability assessments. These activities help participants gain practical experience in detecting vulnerabilities, analyzing threats, and implementing appropriate security controls.

D. Awareness and Mindset Shift: Training programs not only focus on technical skills but also emphasize the importance of cybersecurity awareness and a proactive mindset. Professionals learn to identify social engineering techniques, recognize phishing attempts, and understand the impact of their actions on organizational security. This awareness fosters a culture of security-conscious individuals who actively contribute to a robust cybersecurity posture.

Cybersecurity Education and Academic Programs:

Formal education in cybersecurity offers a comprehensive and structured approach to learning. Academic programs, such as bachelor's and master's degrees in cybersecurity, provide in-depth knowledge in areas such as cryptography, network security, and information assurance. These programs combine theoretical foundations with practical applications, preparing individuals for various roles in the cybersecurity field.

A. Cybersecurity Curricula: Cybersecurity programs typically cover a wide range of topics, including risk management, secure software development, digital forensics, and legal aspects of cybersecurity. These curricula equip students with a broad understanding of the field, enabling them to specialize in specific areas based on their interests and career goals.

B. Research and Innovation: Academic institutions contribute to cybersecurity through research and innovation. Faculty members and students engage in cutting-edge research to develop new defense mechanisms, analyze emerging threats, and propose novel solutions. This research benefits the cybersecurity community by expanding knowledge and informing industry practices.

C. Collaborations and Partnerships: Academic institutions often collaborate with industry partners, government agencies, and cybersecurity organizations to enhance the relevance of their programs. These partnerships provide students with opportunities for internships, industry projects, and access to real-world case studies. Collaborations also facilitate the exchange of knowledge, resources, and expertise between academia and industry, ensuring that cybersecurity education remains up to date and aligned with industry needs.

Continuous Learning and Professional Development:

Cybersecurity is a constantly evolving field, with new threats and attack techniques emerging regularly. Therefore, professionals must engage in continuous learning and professional development to stay abreast of the latest trends and advancements.

A. Ongoing Training Programs: To keep pace with the rapidly changing threat landscape, professionals can participate in ongoing training programs and workshops. These programs provide updates on emerging threats, industry best practices, and new technologies. By continuously updating their skills and knowledge, professionals can adapt their defense strategies and effectively mitigate evolving cyber threats.

B. Industry Conferences and Events: Attending industry conferences, seminars, and events is an excellent way for cybersecurity professionals to expand their network and stay updated on the latest trends. These events often feature renowned speakers, interactive workshops, and opportunities for knowledge sharing and collaboration.

C. Professional Communities and Information Sharing:
Engaging with professional cybersecurity communities, both online and offline, enables professionals to share experiences, learn from peers, and gain insights into real-world challenges and solutions. Online forums, discussion groups, and social media platforms dedicated to cybersecurity provide avenues for information sharing and collaboration.

Building a Cybersecurity Culture:

Training and education in cybersecurity should extend beyond technical professionals. Building a cybersecurity culture across an organization involves educating all employees, regardless of their role or level of technical expertise.

A. Security Awareness Programs: Organizations should implement comprehensive security awareness programs to educate employees about cybersecurity risks, best practices, and their role in protecting sensitive information. Regular training sessions, workshops, and simulated phishing exercises can help raise awareness and promote responsible behavior.

B. Role-Based Training: Different roles within an organization require different levels of cybersecurity knowledge and skills. Tailoring training programs to address specific roles and responsibilities ensures that employees have the necessary expertise to fulfill their cybersecurity obligations effectively.

C. Executive Leadership and Support: Leadership commitment is crucial for establishing a strong cybersecurity culture. Executives and managers should champion cybersecurity initiatives, allocate resources for training, and lead by example in adhering to security protocols.

D. Collaboration and Communication: Fostering collaboration and communication between IT and other departments is essential for building a strong cybersecurity culture. Encouraging open dialogue, sharing success stories and lessons learned, and involving employees in decision-making processes create a sense of collective responsibility towards cybersecurity.

Training and education in cybersecurity are vital for organizations and individuals in the face of ever-evolving cyber threats. By investing in comprehensive training programs, pursuing academic degrees, engaging in continuous learning, and building a cybersecurity culture, professionals can enhance their knowledge, skills, and awareness to protect digital assets effectively. Cybersecurity education not only equips individuals with technical expertise but also fosters a proactive mindset and a culture of security across organizations. With a well-trained and knowledgeable workforce, organizations can mitigate risks, respond effectively to cyber incidents, and maintain a robust defense against the evolving threat landscape. By prioritizing training and education, we empower the defenders of the digital world and contribute to a safer and more secure digital environment for all.

Fostering a Culture of Cybersecurity within an Organization

In today's digital landscape, organizations face constant cyber threats that can lead to data breaches, financial losses, and damage to their reputation. To mitigate these risks, it is crucial for organizations to foster a culture of cybersecurity. This comprehensive book explores the importance of cultivating a cybersecurity culture within an organization and provides practical strategies for achieving this goal. By instilling a shared responsibility for cybersecurity among employees, promoting awareness, and implementing best practices, organizations can create a strong defense against cyber threats.

The Significance of a Cybersecurity Culture:

A. Shared Responsibility: A cybersecurity culture emphasizes that security is not just the responsibility of the IT department, but of every individual within the organization. It encourages employees to take an active role in protecting sensitive information, recognizing potential threats, and reporting suspicious activities.

B. Proactive Mindset: A culture of cybersecurity promotes a proactive rather than reactive approach to security. Employees are encouraged to be vigilant, identify potential risks, and take preventive measures to mitigate them. This mindset helps in identifying and addressing vulnerabilities before they are exploited by malicious actors.

C. Risk Awareness: A cybersecurity culture fosters awareness of the potential risks and consequences of cyber threats. Employees are educated about common attack vectors such as phishing, social engineering, and malware. This knowledge enables them to make informed decisions and exercise caution in their digital interactions.

D. Trust and Confidence: A cybersecurity culture builds trust and confidence among employees, customers, and stakeholders. When individuals see that an organization prioritizes cybersecurity and takes proactive measures to protect their data and privacy, they feel more secure in their interactions with the organization. This trust can enhance the organization's reputation and strengthen relationships with customers and partners.

E. Compliance and Regulatory Requirements: Many industries have specific compliance and regulatory requirements related to data security and privacy. A cybersecurity culture ensures that employees understand and adhere to these requirements, reducing the risk of non-compliance. By embedding security practices into everyday operations, organizations can demonstrate their commitment to compliance and avoid potential legal and financial consequences.

F. Incident Response and Resilience: A cybersecurity culture prepares organizations to effectively respond to security incidents. Employees are trained to identify and report incidents promptly, allowing the organization to take swift action to mitigate the impact. A well-prepared incident response plan, coupled with a culture that encourages proactive reporting, helps minimize damage, shorten recovery time, and enhance overall resilience.

Strategies for Fostering a Cybersecurity Culture:

A. Leadership Commitment: Leadership plays a vital role in shaping the culture of an organization. Executives should demonstrate their commitment to cybersecurity by providing adequate resources, setting an example, and actively participating in security initiatives. This commitment cascades throughout the organization, emphasizing the importance of cybersecurity at all levels.

B. Comprehensive Training and Education: Organizations should invest in comprehensive cybersecurity training and education programs for employees at all levels. This includes raising awareness about common threats, teaching best practices for password management, data handling, and safe browsing habits. Regular training sessions, workshops, and interactive activities can reinforce cybersecurity knowledge.

C. Clear Policies and Procedures: Establishing clear and well-communicated security policies and procedures is essential. Employees should be familiar with acceptable use policies, data protection guidelines, incident reporting procedures, and password requirements. Regular reminders and updates on policies help reinforce their importance.

D. Incident Response Preparedness: Organizations should develop and regularly update an incident response plan to ensure a swift and effective response to cyber incidents. Conducting tabletop exercises and simulations can help test the plan's effectiveness and familiarize employees with their roles and responsibilities during an incident.

E. Continuous Monitoring and Evaluation: Implementing robust monitoring systems enables organizations to detect and respond to potential threats in real-time. Regular security assessments, vulnerability scans, and penetration testing can identify weaknesses and provide opportunities for improvement. Evaluation of security controls and processes helps maintain an effective cybersecurity posture.

Promoting a Secure Work Environment:

A. Secure Access Controls: Implementing strong access controls, including multifactor authentication, role-based access, and regular account reviews, helps protect sensitive data and systems from unauthorized access. Regular access reviews ensure that employees have only the necessary privileges to perform their job responsibilities.

B. Secure Remote Work Practices: With the rise of remote work, organizations should establish guidelines for secure remote access, including the use of virtual private networks (VPNs) and secure communication channels. Employees should be educated on the risks associated with remote work and the steps they can take to mitigate them.

C. Employee Engagement and Communication: Engage employees in cybersecurity initiatives through regular communication, newsletters, and security awareness campaigns. Encourage employees to report security incidents or suspicious activities promptly and provide a safe and confidential reporting mechanism.

D. Recognition and Rewards: Recognize and reward employees who demonstrate exemplary cybersecurity practices or contribute to the improvement of the organization's security posture. This can be done through incentives, certificates of appreciation, or acknowledgement in team meetings. Recognizing employees' efforts reinforces the importance of cybersecurity and motivates others to actively participate.

E. Ongoing Awareness and Training: Cybersecurity threats and attack techniques are constantly evolving. Organizations should provide regular updates and refresher training to employees to keep them informed about the latest trends and emerging threats. This ensures that employees are equipped with the knowledge and skills to adapt to new challenges.

Creating a Secure Organizational Infrastructure:

A. Robust Network Security: Implementing strong network security measures, such as firewalls, intrusion detection systems, and encryption protocols, helps safeguard sensitive data and systems from external threats.

Regular security assessments and network monitoring can identify vulnerabilities and potential breaches.

B. Secure Software Development: Adopt secure coding practices and conduct regular security assessments during the software development lifecycle. Implementing code review processes, penetration testing, and secure coding guidelines can help mitigate vulnerabilities and prevent the introduction of security flaws.

C. Data Protection and Privacy: Organizations should establish data protection policies, including data classification, encryption, and secure storage practices. Regular audits and compliance checks ensure adherence to privacy regulations and protection of sensitive information.

D. Vendor Management: Evaluate the security practices of third-party vendors and partners to ensure they meet the organization's cybersecurity standards. Implementing vendor security assessments and monitoring their compliance with contractual security requirements minimizes potential risks associated with third-party access to systems and data.

E. Incident Reporting and Lessons Learned: Encourage employees to report security incidents promptly and establish a process for capturing and analyzing lessons learned. Conduct post-incident reviews to identify areas for improvement and update security controls and procedures accordingly.

Fostering a culture of cybersecurity within an organization is crucial in today's digital landscape. By emphasizing shared responsibility, promoting awareness, and implementing best practices, organizations can create a strong defense against cyber threats. Through leadership commitment, comprehensive training, clear policies, and a secure work environment, organizations can empower employees to become the first line of defense against cyberattacks. By integrating cybersecurity into the organizational culture, organizations can build resilience, protect sensitive information, and safeguard their reputation in an increasingly interconnected world.

Summary

A proactive approach to cybersecurity is crucial in today's digital landscape to mitigate risks and protect sensitive information. It involves taking preventive measures, staying informed about the latest threats, and implementing security best practices. By adopting a proactive mindset, individuals and organizations can enhance their cybersecurity posture and minimize the impact of cyber threats.

Action Points

1. **Stay Informed:** Keep up-to-date with the latest cybersecurity news, trends, and best practices. Regularly monitor reputable sources, such as cybersecurity organizations and industry blogs, to stay informed about emerging threats and recommended security measures.

2. **Implement Robust Security Measures**: Take proactive steps to protect your digital assets. Install reliable antivirus and antimalware software, use strong and unique passwords, enable two-factor authentication, and keep software and operating systems updated to prevent vulnerabilities that could be exploited by cybercriminals.

3. **Educate and Train Users:** Invest in cybersecurity awareness and training programs to educate employees, family members, or yourself about

potential risks and safe online practices. Ensure that everyone understands the importance of cybersecurity and knows how to identify and respond to common threats like phishing emails or suspicious links.

4. **Regularly Back Up Data:** Implement a regular data backup strategy to safeguard critical information. Store backups in secure and separate locations, both offline and in the cloud, to protect against data loss caused by ransomware attacks, hardware failures, or other unexpected events.

5. **Conduct Security Audits and Assessments:** Regularly assess your cybersecurity measures to identify vulnerabilities and areas for improvement. Perform security audits and penetration tests to evaluate the effectiveness of your security controls and address any weaknesses or gaps in your defenses.

Chapter 3

The Human Element of Cybersecurity - The Role of Technology and The Importance of Education

In the rapidly evolving digital landscape, technology plays a significant role in both enabling and challenging cybersecurity efforts. From sophisticated cyber threats to advanced security solutions, organizations and individuals must leverage technology effectively to protect sensitive information and mitigate risks. However, technology alone is not sufficient. Education and awareness are crucial in empowering individuals to understand the evolving threat landscape and make informed decisions to enhance cybersecurity. This book explores the role of technology and the importance of education in building a strong cybersecurity foundation.

Technology in Cybersecurity

A. Advanced Threats:

1. Discuss the evolving nature of cyber threats, including malware, ransomware, and social

engineering techniques.

2. Highlight the need for advanced technology solutions, such as intrusion detection systems, next-generation firewalls, and artificial intelligence-driven threat intelligence platforms, to combat these threats effectively.

3. Explore the role of technologies like machine learning and behavioral analytics in identifying and responding to emerging threats.

B. Secure Infrastructure:

1. Explain the importance of implementing secure technologies in the organization's infrastructure, such as secure network architecture, encryption, and access controls.

2. Discuss the role of technologies like secure web gateways, endpoint protection, and data loss prevention solutions in safeguarding sensitive data and preventing unauthorized access.

C. Security Automation:

1. Discuss the benefits of security automation tools, such as security information and event management (SIEM) systems, for centralized monitoring and analysis of security events.

2. Highlight the role of automated incident response and threat hunting tools in improving response times and reducing the impact of cyber incidents.

Importance of Education in Cybersecurity

A. Cybersecurity Awareness:

1. Emphasize the significance of educating individuals about cybersecurity risks, best practices, and potential consequences of security breaches.

2. Discuss the role of cybersecurity awareness programs in organizations to promote a culture of security and empower employees to make secure decisions.

B. Training and Skill Development:

1. Highlight the importance of providing comprehensive cybersecurity training and skill development programs for employees.

2. Discuss the various aspects that should be covered in training, including secure coding practices, incident response, and secure configuration management.

C. Cyber Hygiene:

1. Explain the concept of cyber hygiene and its significance in maintaining a secure digital environment.
2. Discuss the importance of educating individuals about password management, software updates, and safe browsing habits to minimize vulnerabilities.

D. Risk Assessment and Management:
1. Explain the role of education in understanding risk assessment methodologies and tools to identify and prioritize potential threats.
2. Discuss the importance of educating individuals on risk management strategies, including incident response planning, business continuity, and disaster recovery.

Technology and Education Synergy

A. Collaboration:
1. Emphasize the need for collaboration between technology experts and educators to develop effective cybersecurity education programs.
2. Discuss the benefits of integrating technology solutions into educational curricula to provide

hands-on experience and practical skills development.

B. Continuous Learning:

1. Highlight the importance of promoting a culture of continuous learning and staying updated on the latest technologies, trends, and best practices in cybersecurity.

2. Discuss the role of professional certifications and ongoing training programs in fostering a mindset of lifelong learning.

C. Security Awareness Tools:

1. Explore the role of technology-enabled security awareness tools, such as simulated phishing campaigns and gamified training platforms, in engaging users and reinforcing cybersecurity knowledge.

2. Discuss how these tools can provide real-time feedback and metrics to measure the effectiveness of education initiatives.

In the battle against cyber threats, technology and education are two pillars that must work together to establish a strong cybersecurity foundation. Technology provides the tools and solutions to detect, prevent, and respond to threats, while education empowers individuals with the knowledge and skills to make informed decisions and protect against evolving risks. By leveraging advanced technologies and investing in comprehensive education initiatives, organizations can build a resilient cybersecurity posture and create a culture of security awareness.

To achieve this synergy between technology and education, organizations should:

1. **Embrace Emerging Technologies:** Stay abreast of the latest advancements in cybersecurity technologies and identify those that align with their organizational needs. Embrace technologies such as artificial intelligence, machine learning, and behavioral analytics to enhance threat detection, automate security processes, and improve incident response capabilities. Embracing emerging technologies is essential for organizations to stay ahead of evolving cyber threats and strengthen their cybersecurity defenses.

   Here's a closer look at how technologies like artificial intelligence (AI), machine learning (ML), and behavioral analytics contribute to enhancing threat detection, automating security processes, and improving incident response capabilities:

a. Artificial Intelligence (AI): AI technologies have revolutionized cybersecurity by enabling advanced threat detection and mitigation. AI algorithms can analyze vast amounts of data, identify patterns, and detect anomalies that may indicate malicious activity. By leveraging AI-powered solutions, organizations can:

- Implement intelligent intrusion detection systems (IDS) and intrusion prevention systems (IPS) that can identify and block potential threats in real-time.

- Utilize AI-based algorithms to analyze network traffic and identify indicators of compromise (IoCs) that may go unnoticed by traditional security systems.

- Deploy AI-driven threat intelligence platforms that collect and analyze threat data from various sources, providing actionable insights to proactively defend against emerging threats.

b. Machine Learning (ML): ML algorithms enable systems to learn from data and adapt their behavior without explicit programming. In the cybersecurity context, ML can be utilized to:

- Develop predictive models that can identify and classify new types of malware based on patterns and behavioral analysis.
- Improve the accuracy of spam filters and email security solutions by learning from user feedback and identifying new patterns of malicious emails.
- Enhance user and entity behavior analytics (UEBA) by creating baselines of normal behavior and detecting anomalies that may indicate insider threats or compromised accounts.

c. Behavioral Analytics: Behavioral analytics focuses on understanding and analyzing user behavior to identify potential security risks. By monitoring patterns of behavior, organizations can:

- Detect insider threats and malicious activity that deviates from normal user behavior.
- Identify unauthorized access attempts or suspicious activities that could indicate compromised accounts or privilege escalation attempts.

- Implement user behavior profiling to detect social engineering attacks, such as phishing or impersonation attempts.

The integration of these technologies into cybersecurity processes brings several advantages, including:

- **Enhanced Threat Detection:** AI, ML, and behavioral analytics enable organizations to identify sophisticated and evolving threats that may bypass traditional security measures. By analyzing vast amounts of data in real-time, these technologies can detect and respond to threats more effectively.

- **Automated Security Processes:** These technologies automate routine security tasks, such as log analysis, threat hunting, and incident response. This frees up security teams to focus on more complex issues and enables faster response times, reducing the impact of security incidents.

- **Improved Incident Response:** AI and ML can help organizations streamline their incident response processes by automating the identification, containment, and remediation of security incidents. By analyzing historical data and learning from past incidents, these technologies can assist in making more informed and efficient response decisions.

- **Reduced False Positives:** ML algorithms can learn to distinguish between legitimate activities and false positives, reducing the number of false alerts and enabling security teams to focus on genuine threats.

Embracing emerging technologies like **AI, ML,** and behavioral analytics empowers organizations to strengthen their cybersecurity posture. By leveraging these technologies, organizations can enhance threat detection, automate security processes, and improve incident response capabilities, ultimately mitigating risks and safeguarding sensitive information from evolving cyber threats.

2. Implement Effective Training Programs: Develop comprehensive training programs that cater to employees at all levels, from basic cybersecurity awareness training for all staff members to specialized technical training for IT and security professionals. These programs should cover a wide range of topics, including best practices for secure email communication, safe browsing habits, password management, and incident response procedures.

Implementing effective training programs is crucial for organizations to empower their employees with the knowledge and skills necessary to protect against cyber threats.

Here's a closer look at developing comprehensive training programs that cater to employees at all levels:

a. Basic Cybersecurity Awareness Training:

    a. Provide all staff members, regardless of their role, with foundational cybersecurity awareness training. This training should cover fundamental concepts, terminology, and best practices to create a baseline understanding of cybersecurity.

    b. Topics to cover may include the importance of strong passwords, recognizing phishing attempts, safe browsing habits, identifying suspicious email attachments, and reporting security incidents.

b. Role-Specific Training:

- Tailor training programs to address the specific cybersecurity challenges and responsibilities of different roles within the organization. For example:

  - **IT and security professionals:** Offer specialized technical training on topics such as network security, secure coding practices, vulnerability management, and incident response.

- **Executives and managers:** Provide training on risk management, compliance requirements, and the role of leadership in promoting a culture of cybersecurity.

- **HR and administrative staff:** Include training on data privacy regulations, handling sensitive information, and the importance of employee onboarding and offboarding processes.

c. Interactive and Engaging Training Methods:

- Utilize a variety of training methods to enhance engagement and knowledge retention. Consider incorporating interactive elements, such as quizzes, simulations, case studies, and real-life examples.

- Provide hands-on exercises and practical demonstrations to reinforce learning and allow participants to apply their knowledge in a controlled environment.

d. Ongoing Training and Refresher Courses:

- Cybersecurity threats and best practices evolve rapidly, so it's essential to provide ongoing training and refresher courses to keep employees up to date.

- Offer periodic training sessions or microlearning

modules that focus on emerging threats, new attack vectors, and industry-specific challenges.

e. Measure and Assess Effectiveness:

- Regularly assess the effectiveness of training programs through feedback surveys, assessments, and simulations.
- Collect data on employee knowledge levels before and after training to evaluate the impact of the training initiatives.
- Use metrics and analytics to identify areas of improvement and adapt the training content accordingly.

f. Promote a Culture of Security:

- Embed cybersecurity into the organizational culture by fostering a mindset of vigilance and accountability.
- Encourage employees to report potential security incidents or suspicious activities promptly.
- Recognize and reward individuals who demonstrate good cybersecurity practices and actively contribute to the security of the organization.

By implementing effective training programs,

organizations can:

- Enhance employees' understanding of cybersecurity risks and best practices.
- Equip employees with the skills to identify and respond to potential threats effectively.
- Foster a culture of security where cybersecurity becomes ingrained in daily work practices.
- Reduce the likelihood of human error leading to security breaches.
- Strengthen the overall cybersecurity posture of the organization.

Remember, ongoing education and training are essential as cybersecurity threats continue to evolve. By investing in comprehensive training programs, organizations can empower their employees to be the first line of defense against cyber threats.

3. Foster a Continuous Learning Culture: Encourage employees to actively participate in ongoing learning and professional development opportunities. Promote the pursuit of cybersecurity certifications and provide resources for self-study and continuous improvement. Foster a culture that values and rewards individuals who demonstrate a commitment to enhancing their cybersecurity knowledge and skills.

Fostering a continuous learning culture within an organization is vital for staying ahead of rapidly evolving cyber threats and maintaining a strong cybersecurity posture.

Here's a deeper exploration of how organizations can promote ongoing learning and professional development in the field of cybersecurity:

a. Encourage Ongoing Learning:

- Emphasize the importance of continuous learning and professional development to employees. Make it clear that cybersecurity is a rapidly changing field and that staying updated is crucial to effectively mitigate risks.

- Encourage employees to dedicate time to self-study, research, and explore new cybersecurity trends, technologies, and best practices.

b. Provide Resources and Support:

- Offer employees access to a variety of resources that facilitate self-study and continuous improvement. These resources may include cybersecurity books, online courses, webinars, and industry publications.

- Provide access to cybersecurity-related tools,

software, and platforms that employees can use for hands-on learning and experimentation.

c. Cybersecurity Certifications:

- Promote the pursuit of industry-recognized cybersecurity certifications. These certifications validate individuals' knowledge and skills in specific cybersecurity domains and demonstrate a commitment to professional development.

- Identify relevant certifications based on job roles and responsibilities, such as Certified Information Systems Security Professional (CISSP), Certified Ethical Hacker (CEH), CompTIA Security+, or Certified Information Security Manager (CISM).

d. Establish a Learning Budget:

- Allocate a budget specifically for cybersecurity training and education. This budget can be used to support employees' enrollment in external training programs, conferences, workshops, or certification exams.

- Demonstrate organizational support for ongoing learning by investing in the professional growth of employees and reinforcing the value placed on cybersecurity knowledge and skills.

e. Foster Knowledge Sharing:

- Encourage employees to share their cybersecurity knowledge and experiences with their colleagues through internal presentations, lunch-and-learn sessions, or dedicated knowledge-sharing platforms.

- Establish a mentorship program where experienced cybersecurity professionals can guide and mentor junior colleagues, fostering knowledge transfer within the organization.

f. Recognize and Reward:

- Establish a recognition and rewards program that acknowledges and celebrates individuals who demonstrate a commitment to enhancing their cybersecurity knowledge and skills.

- Recognize employees who achieve certifications, complete relevant training programs, or contribute to the improvement of the organization's cybersecurity practices.

- Encourage healthy competition by creating friendly challenges or competitions related to cybersecurity knowledge or skills.

By fostering a continuous learning culture, organizations can:

- Ensure that employees stay updated on the latest cybersecurity threats, technologies, and best practices.

- Enable employees to acquire new skills and knowledge that can be applied to their roles, contributing to the overall security posture of the organization.

- Cultivate a sense of ownership and responsibility for cybersecurity among employees, leading to a proactive and vigilant workforce.

- Attract and retain top cybersecurity talent by creating an environment that values professional growth and development.

Cybersecurity is an ever-changing landscape, and organizations must encourage and support continuous learning to adapt to new challenges and effectively protect their digital assets. By promoting ongoing learning and professional development, organizations can foster a culture of cybersecurity excellence and empower their employees to be proactive defenders against cyber threats.

4. Engage with the Cybersecurity Community: Encourage employees to actively engage with the broader cybersecurity community by attending conferences, participating in industry forums, and joining professional associations. This engagement provides opportunities to network, share knowledge, and stay updated on emerging threats, technologies, and best practices.

Engaging with the cybersecurity community is essential for organizations and their employees to stay connected with industry trends, share knowledge, and benefit from collective expertise.

Here's a closer look at the benefits of engaging with the cybersecurity community and how organizations can encourage their employees to actively participate:

a. Networking Opportunities:

- Attending conferences, seminars, and industry events allows employees to network with cybersecurity professionals from different organizations and backgrounds.

- Networking provides opportunities to exchange ideas, collaborate on common challenges, and learn from the experiences of others in the field.

- Engaging with the community can also lead to partnerships, collaborations, and access to resources that can enhance the organization's cybersecurity capabilities.

b. Knowledge Sharing and Learning:

- Participation in cybersecurity forums, online communities, and discussion groups allows employees to share their knowledge and learn from others in the field.

- Employees can gain insights into emerging threats, new attack techniques, and effective cybersecurity practices from experts and practitioners.

- Engaging in discussions and debates fosters critical thinking, challenges assumptions, and promotes continuous learning.

c. Staying Updated on Emerging Threats and Technologies:

- The cybersecurity landscape is constantly evolving, with new threats and technologies emerging regularly.

- Active engagement with the cybersecurity community ensures employees are aware of the latest trends, vulnerabilities, and countermeasures.

- Attending conferences and industry events featuring keynote speakers and experts provides valuable insights into emerging threats, innovative security solutions, and industry best practices.

d. Professional Development Opportunities:

- Many professional associations and industry

organizations offer training programs, webinars, and workshops focused on cybersecurity.

- Encourage employees to participate in these events to enhance their knowledge, develop new skills, and earn relevant certifications.
- Professional development opportunities offered by the cybersecurity community contribute to employees' career growth and increase their value to the organization.

e. Collaboration and Information Sharing:

- Engaging with the cybersecurity community enables organizations to collaborate on shared challenges and exchange information on threat intelligence and incident response.
- Sharing best practices, lessons learned, and case studies with industry peers can help organizations strengthen their security strategies and incident response capabilities.
- Collaboration can extend to participation in industry-wide initiatives, information sharing networks, and public-private partnerships aimed at combating cyber threats collectively.

Organizations can encourage employee engagement with

the cybersecurity community through various means:

- Provide financial support, such as covering conference registration fees or membership dues for professional associations.
- Allocate time for employees to attend industry events, conferences, and webinars.
- Establish internal knowledge-sharing platforms or communities where employees can share insights and experiences with colleagues.
- Recognize and reward employees who actively contribute to the cybersecurity community, such as presenting at conferences or publishing books.

By actively engaging with the cybersecurity community, organizations and their employees can:

- Stay informed about emerging threats, technologies, and best practices.
- Expand their professional network and access valuable resources and expertise.
- Enhance their cybersecurity knowledge and skills through learning from industry peers.
- Collaborate on shared challenges and leverage collective intelligence to improve cybersecurity defenses.

- Contribute to the advancement of the cybersecurity field by sharing insights and experiences with the broader community.

Engagement with the cybersecurity community is a valuable investment in staying updated, fostering innovation, and strengthening the overall cybersecurity posture of the organization. Encouraging employees to actively participate in industry events and connect with their peers fosters a culture of continuous learning and collaboration.

5. Leverage Technology for Education: Integrate technology into educational initiatives to enhance engagement and effectiveness. Utilize interactive e-learning platforms, virtual labs, and gamification techniques to create immersive and interactive learning experiences. Leverage technology-driven assessment tools to evaluate the effectiveness of training programs and identify areas for improvement.

Leveraging technology for education in cybersecurity is crucial for creating engaging and effective learning experiences. By incorporating interactive e-learning platforms, virtual labs, gamification techniques, and assessment tools, organizations can enhance the effectiveness of their training programs.

Here's a deeper exploration of how technology can be utilized for cybersecurity education:

a. Interactive E-Learning Platforms:

- Utilize interactive e-learning platforms that offer multimedia content, videos, interactive modules, and quizzes.

- These platforms allow learners to progress at their own pace, access training materials anytime and anywhere, and provide an engaging learning experience.

- Incorporate real-world scenarios and case studies into the e-learning modules to make the training content relevant and practical.

b. Virtual Labs and Simulations:

- Create virtual lab environments where employees can practice cybersecurity skills in a controlled and risk-free setting.

- Virtual labs enable hands-on learning experiences, allowing participants to explore cybersecurity concepts, perform security assessments, and practice incident response procedures.

- Simulations can simulate realistic cyber attack

scenarios, enabling learners to apply their knowledge and skills in a simulated environment.

c. Gamification Techniques:

- Incorporate gamification elements into training programs to increase engagement and motivation.
- Use game-like features such as leaderboards, badges, rewards, and levels to create a competitive and interactive learning environment.
- Gamification can help reinforce learning, encourage participation, and make the training experience more enjoyable.

d. Technology-Driven Assessment Tools:

- Utilize technology-driven assessment tools to evaluate learners' knowledge, skills, and progress throughout the training program.
- Online quizzes, interactive assessments, and simulations can provide immediate feedback to learners, helping them identify areas for improvement.
- Analyze assessment data to identify knowledge gaps and measure the effectiveness of the training program. This information can guide the refinement and improvement of future training initiatives.

e. Mobile Learning and Microlearning:

- Embrace mobile learning platforms and microlearning approaches to deliver bite-sized cybersecurity training content.

- Mobile learning allows employees to access training materials on their smartphones or tablets, enabling learning on-the-go and accommodating different learning styles.

- Microlearning breaks down complex topics into short, focused modules, making it easier for learners to digest information and retain knowledge.

f. Data Analytics and Personalized Learning:

- Leverage data analytics to gain insights into learners' progress, engagement levels, and learning preferences.

- Personalize the learning experience by recommending tailored training modules based on individual needs and skill gaps.

- Use data analytics to identify trends and patterns, enabling organizations to continuously improve the effectiveness of their training programs.

By leveraging technology for education in cybersecurity, organizations can:

- Enhance learner engagement, motivation, and

knowledge retention through interactive and immersive learning experiences.

- Provide flexible learning opportunities that can be accessed anytime and anywhere, accommodating different schedules and learning preferences.

- Facilitate hands-on practice and simulations to develop practical cybersecurity skills.

- Assess learner progress and identify areas for improvement using technology-driven assessment tools.

- Personalize the learning experience to address individual needs and optimize training outcomes.

Technology should be seen as an enabler in cybersecurity education, enhancing the learning experience and ensuring that training programs remain relevant, engaging, and effective in addressing the evolving cybersecurity landscape.

The role of technology and the importance of education are intertwined when it comes to building a robust cybersecurity framework. Organizations must leverage advanced technologies to detect and respond to evolving threats, while also investing in comprehensive education initiatives to empower individuals with the knowledge and skills to make informed decisions and contribute to a secure digital environment. By embracing the synergy between technology and education, organizations can establish a strong cybersecurity culture, mitigate risks, and protect sensitive information in an increasingly complex threat landscape.

Tips on Social Media Privacy Settings, Encryption, and Secure Communication Tools

1. Social Media Privacy Settings:

- Regularly review and adjust your privacy settings on social media platforms to control what information is visible to others.

- Limit the audience for your posts and profile information to trusted friends and connections.

- Be cautious about sharing personal information such as your full name, address, phone number, or birthdate on public profiles.

- Disable location tracking features that reveal your whereabouts.

- Regularly review and remove any unnecessary or outdated information from your social media profiles.

2. Two-Factor Authentication (2FA):

- Enable two-factor authentication for your social media accounts whenever possible. This adds an extra layer of security by requiring a second verification step, such as a unique code sent to your mobile device, in addition to your password.

- Use an authenticator app or hardware key for **2FA** instead of relying solely on SMS-based verification, as **SMS** can be vulnerable to *SIM swapping attacks*.

3. Encryption for Messaging and Calls:

- Use messaging apps that offer end-to-end encryption, which ensures that only the intended recipients can access the contents of your messages. Popular encrypted messaging apps include Signal, WhatsApp (with *"Signal Protocol"* enabled), and Telegram (with *"Secret Chats"* enabled).

- Consider using voice and video calling apps that employ end-to-end encryption, such as Signal or WhatsApp, to protect your conversations from eavesdropping.

4. Secure Email Communication:

- Opt for email providers that support encryption, such as *ProtonMail* or *Tutanota*, which offer end-to-end encryption for your emails.

- When sending sensitive information via email, use password-protected files or encrypted file-sharing services instead of attaching files directly to the email.

- Be cautious of phishing emails and avoid clicking on suspicious links or downloading attachments from unknown senders.

5. Virtual Private Networks (VPNs):

- Use a reputable **VPN** service when connecting to public Wi-Fi networks or accessing the internet from untrusted locations. A **VPN** encrypts your internet traffic, protecting your data from interception and ensuring your online activities remain private.

- Choose a **VPN** provider that does not log your browsing history and has strong encryption protocols.

6. Secure File Storage and Sharing:

- Use secure cloud storage services that offer encryption for your files, both at rest and during transit. Examples include Dropbox (with *"Dropbox Vault"* enabled), Google Drive (with *"Advanced Protection"* enabled), or *Sync.com*.

- When sharing files, consider using password-protected archives or encrypted file-sharing services, such as *Tresorit* or *Mega*.

7. Keep Software and Devices Updated:

- Regularly update your operating system, applications, and devices to ensure you have the latest security patches and bug fixes.
- Enable automatic updates whenever possible to ensure timely installation of security updates.

8. Strong, Unique Passwords:

- Use strong, unique passwords for your social media accounts and online services. Avoid using easily guessable information such as birthdates or common phrases.
- Consider using a password manager to securely store and generate complex passwords for different accounts.

9. Be Mindful of Third-Party Apps:

- Review the permissions requested by third-party applications before granting access to your social media accounts. Be cautious of apps that request excessive access to your personal information.
- Regularly review and revoke access for apps that you no longer use or trust.

10. Public Wi-Fi Precautions:

- Avoid accessing sensitive information or logging

into your social media accounts when connected to public Wi-Fi networks, as they can be insecure and prone to eavesdropping. If necessary, use a VPN for added security.

Remember, while implementing these tips can enhance your privacy and security on social media, it's important to stay vigilant and practice good digital hygiene. Regularly review and update your privacy

Government and Corporate Responsibility in Protecting Privacy

In today's digital age, where personal information is collected and processed on a massive scale, both governments and corporations have a responsibility to protect individuals' privacy. *Safeguarding privacy* is essential to maintain trust, uphold fundamental rights, and ensure the responsible use of personal data.

Let's explore the role of governments and corporations in protecting privacy and the measures they can take to fulfill this responsibility:

Government Responsibility:

1. Legislation and Regulation:

- Governments should enact comprehensive privacy laws and regulations that provide clear guidelines for the collection, storage, and use of personal data.

- These laws should include provisions for informed consent, data minimization, purpose limitation, data accuracy, security safeguards, and individuals' rights to access, correct, and delete their personal information.

- Governments should establish independent regulatory bodies to oversee compliance with privacy laws and enforce penalties for non-compliance.

2. International Cooperation:

- Governments should collaborate at the international level to develop common standards and frameworks for privacy protection.

- Cross-border data transfer mechanisms should be established to ensure that personal information is adequately protected when it flows across jurisdictions.

- Governments should work together to combat global privacy threats, such as cybercrime and surveillance, through information sharing, capacity building, and joint enforcement efforts.

3. Education and Awareness:

- Governments should invest in public education campaigns to raise awareness about privacy rights and best practices for protecting personal information.

- Educational initiatives should target individuals, businesses, and other stakeholders to promote a culture of privacy-conscious behavior.

4. Surveillance Oversight:

- Governments should establish robust oversight mechanisms to ensure that surveillance activities are conducted lawfully, proportionately, and with appropriate safeguards.

- Judicial authorization and independent review should be required for intrusive surveillance measures.

- Transparency reports should be published to provide information about the scope and nature of government surveillance activities.

Corporate Responsibility:

1. Privacy by Design:

- Corporations should adopt privacy by design principles, embedding privacy considerations into their products, services, and business processes from the outset.

- Privacy impact assessments should be conducted to identify and mitigate privacy risks associated with data collection, processing, storage, and sharing.

2. Data Minimization and Purpose Limitation:

- Corporations should collect and retain only the necessary personal data for legitimate purposes.

- Clear data retention policies should be implemented to ensure that personal information is not kept longer than required.

3. Security Measures:

- Corporations should implement robust security measures to protect personal data from unauthorized access, disclosure, alteration, or destruction.

- Encryption, access controls, regular security audits,

and incident response plans should be in place to mitigate the risk of data breaches.

4. Transparent Data Practices:

- Corporations should provide clear and easily accessible privacy policies that explain how personal data is collected, used, shared, and protected.

- Individuals should be informed about the types of data collected, the purposes for which it is used, and any third parties with whom it is shared.

5. Individual Rights:

- Corporations should respect individuals' rights to access, correct, and delete their personal information.

- Robust mechanisms should be in place to handle individuals' requests and address privacy concerns.

6. Employee Training and Awareness:

- Corporations should provide regular privacy training and awareness programs to employees to ensure they understand their responsibilities in handling personal data.

- Privacy policies and guidelines should be communicated effectively to all employees.

7. Third-Party Data Sharing:

- When sharing personal data with third parties, corporations should ensure that appropriate data protection agreements are in place to safeguard individuals' privacy rights.

- Due diligence should be conducted when engaging third-party service providers to ensure they have adequate privacy and security measures in place.

8. Accountability and Compliance:

- Corporations should establish privacy governance frameworks and designate privacy officers or data protection officers to oversee privacy compliance.

- Regular audits and assessments should be conducted to ensure ongoing compliance with privacy laws and regulations.

- Corporations should maintain records of their data processing activities and be prepared to demonstrate compliance upon request.

9. Transparency and Accountability:

- Corporations should be transparent about their data practices and be accountable for how they handle personal information.

- Regularly publishing transparency reports or

privacy impact assessments can help build trust with consumers and stakeholders.

- Corporations should be responsive to privacy-related inquiries and complaints, providing individuals with avenues to address their concerns.

10. Collaboration between Governments and Corporations:

- Effective protection of privacy requires collaboration between governments and corporations. They should work together to establish common standards, share best practices, and address emerging privacy challenges.
- Governments can provide guidance and support to corporations in implementing privacy measures, while corporations can contribute their expertise and insights to help shape effective regulations.

11. Promoting Privacy-Enhancing Technologies:

- Governments and corporations should promote the development and adoption of privacy-enhancing technologies.
- Investing in research and development of privacy-preserving solutions, such as differential privacy, homomorphic encryption, and decentralized

identity systems, can help protect personal data while enabling valuable services.

12. Data Breach Notification and Incident Response:

- Both governments and corporations should have robust data breach notification and incident response procedures in place. In the event of a data breach, timely notification to affected individuals allows them to take necessary precautions to protect themselves.

- Corporations should have well-defined incident response plans to minimize the impact of a breach and ensure a swift and effective response.

13. International Cooperation and Harmonization:

- Given the global nature of data flows, governments and corporations should work towards harmonizing privacy laws and regulations across jurisdictions.

- International cooperation is crucial to address challenges associated with cross-border data transfers and ensure consistent protection of individuals' privacy rights.

14. Ongoing Evaluation and Improvement:

- Both governments and corporations should continuously evaluate and improve their privacy practices.

- Regular assessments, audits, and reviews can help identify areas for improvement and ensure that privacy measures remain effective in the face of evolving threats and technologies.

Protecting privacy is a shared responsibility between governments and corporations. Governments play a vital role in establishing and enforcing privacy laws and regulations, while corporations must prioritize privacy by design, transparency, and accountability in their data handling practices. By working together, governments and corporations can create a privacy-conscious ecosystem that respects individuals' rights, builds trust, and enables responsible innovation in the digital age.

Summary

The human element of cybersecurity recognizes that people play a critical role in maintaining a secure digital environment. Despite advanced technologies and security measures, human behavior and actions can significantly impact cybersecurity. Understanding and addressing the human element is essential to strengthen overall security.

It involves promoting cybersecurity awareness, educating users, fostering a culture of security, and empowering individuals to make informed decisions.

Action Points

1. **Cybersecurity Awareness Training:** Provide comprehensive cybersecurity awareness training to all individuals within an organization or household. Educate them about common cyber threats, social engineering techniques, and safe online practices. Encourage them to adopt security-conscious behaviors and be vigilant in recognizing and reporting potential security incidents.

2. **Strong Password and Authentication Practices:** Emphasize the importance of using strong and unique passwords for all online accounts. Encourage the use of password managers to generate and store complex passwords securely. Implement multi-factor authentication (MFA) to add an extra layer of security and protect against unauthorized access.

3. **Phishing Awareness and Email Hygiene:** Raise

awareness about phishing attacks and teach individuals how to identify suspicious emails, links, and attachments. Encourage skepticism and verify the authenticity of requests for personal information or sensitive data. Promote email hygiene practices, such as not clicking on unknown links and reporting suspicious emails.

4. **Foster a Culture of Security:** Create a culture where cybersecurity is valued and prioritized. Encourage open communication about security concerns, provide channels for reporting incidents, and reward individuals for practicing good security habits. Regularly communicate cybersecurity updates, reminders, and best practices to maintain awareness and engagement.

5. **Continuous Education and Adaptation:** Cybersecurity is a rapidly evolving field, and it is crucial to stay updated on emerging threats, vulnerabilities, and best practices. Encourage continuous education by attending webinars, workshops, or conferences related to cybersecurity. Stay informed about the latest security technologies, trends, and regulations to adapt security measures

accordingly.

Chapter 4

Real-world Examples and Case Studies - Illustrations of the Importance of Cybersecurity

In today's interconnected digital world, the importance of cybersecurity cannot be overstated. Cyber threats pose significant risks to individuals, businesses, and even nations. The following illustrations highlight the criticality of cybersecurity and why it is essential to protect our digital assets:

1. Protecting Personal Information: Personal information, such as social security numbers, financial details, and healthcare records, is highly valuable to cybercriminals. Without robust cybersecurity measures in place, individuals become vulnerable to identity theft, financial fraud, and other malicious activities. Cybersecurity ensures the confidentiality, integrity, and availability of personal data, safeguarding individuals' privacy and preventing potential harm.

In today's interconnected world, protecting personal information is of paramount importance. Cybercriminals are constantly devising new and sophisticated ways to exploit vulnerabilities and gain unauthorized access to sensitive data. Without robust cybersecurity measures in place, individuals' personal information becomes a prime target, exposing them to various risks such as identity theft, financial fraud, and privacy breaches.

One of the fundamental aspects of cybersecurity is ensuring the confidentiality of personal data. Confidentiality refers to limiting access to information only to authorized individuals or entities. Encryption techniques, secure communication channels, and access controls are essential components of safeguarding personal information. By encrypting data, sensitive information is transformed into an unreadable format, making it nearly impossible for unauthorized individuals to decipher. Secure communication channels, such as virtual private networks (VPNs), protect data as it is transmitted over the internet, preventing interception and unauthorized access.

Maintaining the integrity of personal information is another crucial aspect of cybersecurity. Integrity ensures that data remains accurate, complete, and unaltered. Cybercriminals may attempt to manipulate or modify personal data for their malicious purposes, such as altering financial records or falsifying identities. Implementing measures like data validation, checksums, and digital signatures can help detect any unauthorized changes to personal information. Regular data backups and secure storage practices are also essential to protect against data loss or corruption.

Availability of personal information refers to ensuring that individuals have timely and uninterrupted access to their own data when needed. Cybersecurity measures aim to prevent disruptions caused by cyberattacks, system failures, or other incidents that may render personal information inaccessible. Redundancy, backup systems, and disaster recovery plans are critical in maintaining the availability of personal data, ensuring that individuals can retrieve their information when required.

Moreover, cybersecurity also involves educating individuals about best practices for protecting their personal information. This includes promoting strong and unique passwords, enabling multi-factor authentication, and being cautious of phishing attempts and suspicious links. Regularly updating software and operating systems, using reputable antivirus and anti-malware programs, and being mindful of privacy settings on social media platforms are additional measures individuals can take to enhance their cybersecurity.

On a broader scale, governments play a crucial role in protecting personal information. They enact legislation and regulations that set standards for the handling and protection of personal data by organizations. Data protection laws, such as the General Data Protection Regulation (GDPR) in the European Union, impose strict obligations on businesses regarding the collection, processing, and storage of personal information. Governments also establish regulatory bodies that oversee compliance and enforce penalties for data breaches or privacy violations.

Protecting personal information is a vital aspect of cybersecurity. It involves ensuring the confidentiality, integrity, and availability of personal data, safeguarding individuals' privacy, and mitigating the risks of identity theft, financial fraud, and privacy breaches. By implementing robust cybersecurity measures, individuals and organizations can create a secure digital environment where personal information is safeguarded, promoting trust, confidence, and a safer online experience for all.

2. Safeguarding Business Operations: For organizations, cybersecurity is crucial for protecting critical business operations and assets. Cyberattacks can disrupt business activities, compromise sensitive information, and cause financial losses. From intellectual property theft to ransomware attacks, businesses face a range of cyber threats that can significantly impact their reputation and bottom line. Implementing robust cybersecurity measures helps safeguard business continuity, customer trust, and competitive advantage.

In today's digital landscape, businesses heavily rely on technology and interconnected systems to conduct their operations efficiently and effectively. However, this reliance also exposes them to various cyber threats and risks that can disrupt business operations and compromise sensitive information. Safeguarding business operations through cybersecurity measures is essential to protect against these threats and ensure continuity, customer trust, and competitive advantage.

One of the primary concerns for businesses is the protection of sensitive data and intellectual property. Cybercriminals are constantly seeking to gain unauthorized access to valuable information, such as customer data, trade secrets, financial records, and proprietary technology. Intellectual property theft can result in significant financial losses, damage to reputation, and loss of competitive advantage. Implementing strong security controls, access restrictions, and encryption techniques can help protect sensitive data from unauthorized access and mitigate the risk of intellectual property theft.

Another critical aspect of safeguarding business operations is ensuring the availability and reliability of systems and services. Cyberattacks, such as distributed *denial-of-service (DDoS) attacks*, can overwhelm systems, leading to service disruptions and downtime. This can have severe consequences, including lost productivity, revenue losses, and damage to customer trust. Implementing measures such as network redundancy, load balancing, and intrusion detection systems can help detect and mitigate potential disruptions, ensuring the availability and continuity of business operations.

Protecting customer trust is vital for businesses to maintain a competitive edge and sustain long-term success. Customers expect their personal information to be handled with care and protected from unauthorized access or disclosure. Data breaches can erode customer trust and loyalty, leading to reputational damage and potential loss of business. By implementing robust cybersecurity measures, businesses demonstrate their commitment to safeguarding customer data, building trust, and maintaining a positive reputation in the marketplace.

Cybersecurity also plays a crucial role in ensuring regulatory compliance for businesses. Depending on the industry and geographical location, businesses may be subject to specific data protection and privacy regulations. Non-compliance with these regulations can result in significant fines, legal penalties, and damage to the organization's reputation. By implementing adequate cybersecurity measures, businesses can demonstrate their commitment to meeting regulatory requirements and protecting the privacy and rights of individuals.

Furthermore, cybersecurity is essential for securing supply chains and business partnerships. Businesses often collaborate with suppliers, vendors, and partners to deliver products and services. Weak cybersecurity practices within the supply chain can expose businesses to vulnerabilities and risks. Implementing robust cybersecurity measures, such as conducting third-party risk assessments, establishing secure communication channels, and enforcing data protection agreements, helps mitigate the risk of cyber threats and ensures the integrity and security of the entire business ecosystem.

Safeguarding business operations through cybersecurity measures is crucial in today's digital landscape. By protecting sensitive data and intellectual property, ensuring the availability and reliability of systems, maintaining customer trust, meeting regulatory requirements, and securing supply chains, businesses can mitigate the risks posed by cyber threats. Implementing a comprehensive cybersecurity strategy enables organizations to protect their assets, maintain business continuity, and foster a secure and trusted environment for their customers and stakeholders.

3. Preserving National Security: Cybersecurity plays a vital role in preserving national security. Governments, military organizations, and critical infrastructure sectors are prime targets for cyber threats. State-sponsored cyber espionage, ransomware attacks on infrastructure, and information warfare can have severe implications for a nation's security and economy. A strong cybersecurity posture is essential for protecting sensitive government information, defending against cyber warfare, and ensuring the stability of national infrastructure.

The preservation of national security is closely intertwined with cybersecurity. Governments, military organizations, and critical infrastructure sectors face a growing number of cyber threats that have the potential to cause significant damage to national security, economy, and public safety. The importance of cybersecurity in preserving national security cannot be overstated, and several key factors highlight its significance.

4. Protection of Sensitive Government Information: Governments hold vast amounts of sensitive information related to national security, intelligence, defense strategies, and diplomatic communications. This information is highly valuable to adversaries who seek to gain unauthorized access to classified data for political, economic, or military advantage. Robust cybersecurity measures, such as secure network architectures, encryption, and strong access controls, are necessary to protect sensitive government information from cyber espionage and unauthorized disclosure.

5. Defending Against Cyber Warfare: Cyber warfare has emerged as a prominent threat in the modern era.

State-sponsored cyber attacks targeting critical infrastructure, military systems, and government networks pose significant risks to national security. These attacks can disrupt essential services, compromise military capabilities, and destabilize a nation's infrastructure. A strong cybersecurity posture, including advanced threat detection systems, incident response capabilities, and cyber defense strategies, is essential for effectively detecting, mitigating, and responding to cyber warfare threats.

6. Securing Critical Infrastructure: Critical infrastructure sectors, such as energy, transportation, healthcare, and finance, are essential for the functioning of a nation's economy and public welfare. These sectors are prime targets for cyber attacks due to their interconnectedness and reliance on technology systems. A successful attack on critical infrastructure can have far-reaching consequences, including widespread disruptions, economic losses, and threats to public safety. Implementing robust cybersecurity measures within critical infrastructure sectors is crucial for preventing and mitigating cyber threats, ensuring the availability and integrity of essential services, and safeguarding national security.

7. Protection of Defense Systems and Military Operations: The military relies heavily on interconnected systems and advanced technologies to execute operations, gather intelligence, and maintain situational awareness. Cyber attacks targeting defense systems and military networks can undermine operational capabilities, compromise classified information, and disrupt military operations. Strong cybersecurity measures, including secure communications channels, network segmentation, and continuous monitoring, are vital for protecting defense systems, ensuring operational readiness, and safeguarding national security interests.

8. Cyber Intelligence and Information Sharing: Effective cybersecurity in the context of national security requires robust cyber intelligence capabilities and information sharing mechanisms. Governments and security agencies must have the ability to gather intelligence on emerging cyber threats, identify threat actors, and analyze their tactics, techniques, and procedures. Timely and actionable intelligence enables proactive defense measures, threat mitigation, and the sharing of critical information with other government entities and international partners, facilitating a collective response to cyber threats.

9. International Cooperation: Preserving national security in cyberspace requires international cooperation and collaboration. Cyber threats do not respect national borders, and adversaries can launch attacks from anywhere in the world. Governments must work together to establish common frameworks, information-sharing mechanisms, and legal frameworks to combat cyber threats effectively. International cooperation facilitates the exchange of best practices, intelligence sharing, joint cyber exercises, and the development of norms of behavior in cyberspace, enhancing global cybersecurity and preserving national security interests.

The preservation of national security in the digital age relies heavily on robust cybersecurity measures. Protecting sensitive government information, defending against cyber warfare, securing critical infrastructure, safeguarding defense systems and military operations, promoting cyber intelligence and information sharing, and fostering international cooperation are all critical components of a comprehensive cybersecurity strategy.

By investing in cybersecurity capabilities and adopting a proactive approach to cyber threats, governments can enhance national security, protect public welfare, and safeguard the interests of their citizens.

Ensuring Economic Stability:

A secure digital environment is crucial for economic stability and growth. Cyberattacks targeting financial institutions, online marketplaces, and e-commerce platforms can disrupt financial systems, erode consumer trust, and undermine economic stability. Effective cybersecurity measures protect financial transactions, secure online transactions, and foster a secure environment for digital trade, thereby bolstering economic resilience and facilitating innovation.

In the digital age, ensuring economic stability goes hand in hand with maintaining a secure digital environment. Cybersecurity plays a vital role in protecting financial institutions, online marketplaces, and e-commerce platforms from cyber threats that can disrupt economic systems, compromise consumer trust, and hinder economic growth. Here's why cybersecurity is crucial for economic stability:

2. Protection of Financial Transactions: With the rise of online banking and digital payment systems, secure financial transactions have become a cornerstone of economic activity. Cybercriminals target financial institutions, credit card information, and personal financial data in their attempts to commit fraud, identity theft, and financial crimes. Robust cybersecurity measures, such as strong encryption, multi-factor authentication, and secure network infrastructure, are essential to protect financial transactions and prevent unauthorized access to sensitive financial information. By safeguarding financial transactions, cybersecurity helps maintain the trust and confidence necessary for a stable and thriving economy.

3. Security of Online Marketplaces: Online marketplaces have transformed the way businesses operate, allowing them to reach a global customer base and facilitate seamless transactions. However, these platforms are attractive targets for cybercriminals seeking to exploit vulnerabilities and compromise customer data. Breaches in online marketplaces can lead to the theft of customer information, including payment details and personal data, resulting in financial losses, reputational damage, and diminished consumer trust. Robust cybersecurity measures, such as secure website protocols, encryption, and continuous monitoring, help protect online marketplaces, ensuring the integrity of transactions and fostering a secure environment for digital commerce.

4. Consumer Confidence and Trust: Economic stability relies on consumer confidence and trust in digital systems and platforms. When consumers feel that their personal and financial information is secure, they are more likely to engage in online transactions, making purchases, and conducting business digitally. Cybersecurity measures, such as secure communication channels, transparent data practices, and effective privacy protection, are crucial for building and maintaining consumer trust. By establishing a secure digital environment, cybersecurity fosters consumer confidence, encourages economic activity, and supports long-term economic stability.

5. Preventing Economic Disruption: Cyberattacks can have far-reaching consequences for businesses and the overall economy. Ransomware attacks, distributed denial-of-service (DDoS) attacks, and other cyber threats can disrupt critical business operations, leading to financial losses, service interruptions, and supply chain disruptions.

These disruptions can have a cascading effect on the economy, impacting multiple industries, businesses, and stakeholders. Robust cybersecurity measures, including proactive threat detection, incident response plans, and disaster recovery strategies, help prevent and mitigate the impact of cyberattacks, ensuring the continuity of business operations and preserving economic stability.

6. Facilitating Innovation and Digital Transformation: A secure digital environment is essential for fostering innovation and supporting digital transformation efforts. Businesses and industries are increasingly reliant on digital technologies, cloud computing, and data analytics to drive growth and competitiveness. However, the rapid adoption of these technologies also introduces new vulnerabilities and cybersecurity risks. By implementing strong cybersecurity practices, organizations can confidently embrace digital transformation, harness the power of emerging technologies, and drive innovation while mitigating the potential risks associated with cyber threats. This, in turn, enables businesses to adapt to changing market dynamics, remain competitive, and contribute to economic stability.

Cybersecurity plays a crucial role in ensuring economic

stability in the digital age. By protecting financial transactions, securing online marketplaces, fostering consumer confidence and trust, preventing economic disruption, and facilitating innovation and digital transformation, cybersecurity provides a solid foundation for economic growth and resilience. Governments, businesses, and individuals must prioritize cybersecurity measures to safeguard economic systems, support digital commerce, and maintain the stability and integrity of the global economy.

Mitigating Cybercrime and Fraud:

Cybercrime is a growing threat that costs individuals and businesses billions of dollars each year. Cybercriminals employ various techniques, such as phishing, malware, and social engineering, to defraud unsuspecting victims. Robust cybersecurity measures, such as multi-factor authentication, encryption, and intrusion detection systems, help mitigate cybercrime and fraud, protecting individuals and organizations from financial losses and reputational damage.

Mitigating cybercrime and fraud is a critical aspect of

cybersecurity that plays a significant role in protecting individuals, businesses, and society as a whole. Cybercriminals employ sophisticated techniques and strategies to exploit vulnerabilities and deceive unsuspecting victims.

Here's why cybersecurity is crucial in mitigating cybercrime and fraud:

1. Protection against Phishing Attacks: Phishing attacks are one of the most common and effective methods used by cybercriminals to trick individuals into revealing sensitive information, such as login credentials, credit card details, or personal identification information. These attacks are typically carried out through deceptive emails, fake websites, or social media messages that appear legitimate. Effective cybersecurity measures, such as email filtering, anti-phishing software, and user awareness training, help detect and block phishing attempts, reducing the risk of individuals falling victim to these fraudulent schemes.

2. Prevention of Malware Infections: Malware, including viruses, ransomware, and spyware, is a significant threat to individuals and organizations. It can be distributed through malicious email attachments, infected websites, or compromised software. Once installed on a device or network, malware can cause significant harm, including data breaches, financial loss, and unauthorized access to sensitive information. Robust cybersecurity measures, such as anti-malware software, regular system updates, and secure browsing practices, help prevent and detect malware infections, reducing the risk of cybercrime and fraud.

3. Detection of Social Engineering Techniques: Social engineering involves manipulating individuals to disclose sensitive information or perform certain actions that benefit the cybercriminal. Techniques like pretexting, baiting, and impersonation are commonly used in social engineering attacks. By building a cybersecurity-aware culture and providing comprehensive training, organizations can empower employees to recognize and report social engineering attempts, preventing fraud and unauthorized access to confidential data.

4. Secure Online Transactions: E-commerce and online banking have revolutionized the way we conduct financial transactions. However, these transactions also present opportunities for cybercriminals to intercept sensitive information, such as credit card details or banking credentials. Implementing secure communication protocols, such as *Transport Layer Security (TLS),* and utilizing encryption technologies ensure that data exchanged during online transactions remains confidential and inaccessible to unauthorized individuals.

5. Fraud Detection and Monitoring: Organizations can employ advanced cybersecurity tools and technologies to detect and monitor fraudulent activities in real-time. Machine learning algorithms, anomaly detection systems, and behavioral analytics can identify patterns and deviations that indicate potential fraud. By leveraging these technologies, businesses can promptly respond to suspicious activities, preventing financial losses and reputational damage.

6. Collaboration and Information Sharing: Government agencies, law enforcement bodies, and private organizations can collaborate and share information to combat cybercrime effectively. Sharing threat intelligence, best practices, and attack trends can help identify emerging threats, detect patterns, and develop proactive strategies to mitigate cybercrime and fraud. Public-private partnerships and information-sharing initiatives contribute to a collective defense against cybercriminals and enhance overall cybersecurity.

Mitigating cybercrime and fraud is a fundamental aspect of cybersecurity. By implementing robust security measures, raising awareness, leveraging advanced technologies, and fostering collaboration, individuals and organizations can protect themselves against cyber threats. It is essential to stay vigilant, adopt best practices, and continuously adapt security measures to counter evolving cybercriminal tactics. By doing so, we can create a safer digital environment and minimize the impact of cybercrime and fraud on individuals, businesses, and society as a whole.

Preserving Intellectual Property:

Innovation and intellectual property (IP) are the lifeblood of many organizations. Cyberattacks targeting IP theft can result in the loss of valuable research, development, and competitive advantage. Cybersecurity measures such as data encryption, access controls, and IP protection strategies are crucial for safeguarding proprietary information and fostering a climate of innovation.

Preserving intellectual property (IP) is a critical aspect of cybersecurity that directly impacts the competitiveness and success of organizations. Intellectual property includes patents, trade secrets, copyrights, and trademarks, which are valuable assets that drive innovation, growth, and market differentiation.

Here's why cybersecurity is essential in preserving intellectual property:

Protection against IP Theft: Cybercriminals and state-sponsored actors target organizations to steal valuable intellectual property. They employ various tactics, including hacking, phishing, and insider threats, to gain unauthorized access to sensitive information. Robust cybersecurity measures, such as data encryption, access controls, and intrusion detection systems, help prevent unauthorized access and protect IP from theft.

Safeguarding Research and Development: Research and development (R&D) efforts are a significant investment for organizations, and the results often represent valuable intellectual property. Cyberattacks targeting R&D departments aim to steal research findings, product designs, formulas, algorithms, and other confidential information. By implementing strong cybersecurity measures, organizations can protect their R&D assets, maintain a competitive edge, and ensure the continued success of their innovation initiatives.

Preventing Industrial Espionage: In highly competitive industries, industrial espionage is a constant threat. Cybercriminals, competitors, or foreign entities may attempt to infiltrate an organization's network to gather strategic information, trade secrets, or other proprietary data. Robust cybersecurity measures, including network segmentation, intrusion detection, and security monitoring, can detect and prevent unauthorized access, thwarting attempts at industrial espionage.

Securing Collaboration and Partnerships:

Organizations often collaborate with partners, vendors, and suppliers to drive innovation and bring products or services to market. These collaborations involve sharing sensitive information and intellectual property. Implementing secure collaboration platforms, establishing secure data sharing protocols, and enforcing contractual obligations can help protect shared IP and maintain trust among partners.

Encryption and Data Protection: Encryption plays a vital role in protecting intellectual property. By encrypting data at rest and in transit, organizations ensure that even if the information is intercepted, it remains unreadable and useless to unauthorized individuals. Strong encryption algorithms, key management practices, and secure storage solutions contribute to the overall protection of IP assets.

Implementing Access Controls: Implementing access controls is essential to restrict unauthorized access to intellectual property. Role-based access controls, strong authentication mechanisms, and privilege management help ensure that only authorized personnel can access and modify sensitive IP. This reduces the risk of internal threats and accidental exposure of valuable information.

Employee Awareness and Training: Educating

employees about the importance of protecting intellectual property and implementing proper security practices is crucial. Employees should be aware of the value of IP, the risks of data breaches, and the importance of following security protocols. Regular training programs, security awareness campaigns, and policies that govern the handling of intellectual property create a culture of responsibility and contribute to its protection.

Monitoring and Incident Response: Implementing robust monitoring and incident response capabilities is essential for detecting and responding to potential IP breaches. Security monitoring tools, log analysis, and threat intelligence can help identify suspicious activities and potential IP theft. Incident response plans should be in place to facilitate a swift and effective response to any security incidents involving intellectual property.

Preserving intellectual property requires a comprehensive cybersecurity strategy. By implementing robust security measures, raising awareness, securing collaborations, and prioritizing data protection, organizations can safeguard their valuable intellectual property. Protecting IP contributes to innovation, competitiveness, and the long-term success of organizations in today's digital landscape.

Protecting Critical Infrastructure:

Critical infrastructure, including power grids, transportation systems, and healthcare facilities, relies heavily on interconnected networks and technology. A breach in cybersecurity can have catastrophic consequences, leading to disruptions in essential services and compromising public safety. Robust cybersecurity measures, including network segmentation, intrusion detection systems, and incident response plans, are critical for protecting critical infrastructure from cyber threats and ensuring the continuity of essential services.

Protecting critical infrastructure is a paramount concern in cybersecurity, as the consequences of a successful cyberattack can be severe and widespread.

Here's an elaboration on why robust cybersecurity measures are essential for safeguarding critical infrastructure:

Dependence on Interconnected Networks: Critical infrastructure systems, such as power grids, water treatment plants, and transportation networks, rely on interconnected networks for their operations. These networks enable real-time monitoring, control, and data exchange, enhancing efficiency and effectiveness. However, they also create vulnerabilities that can be exploited by cybercriminals. Robust cybersecurity measures, including network segmentation and secure access controls, help isolate critical systems from potential threats and limit the impact of a cyberattack.

Protection against Disruptions: Disruptions in critical infrastructure can have severe consequences for public safety, the economy, and national security. For example, a cyberattack targeting a power grid can result in widespread power outages, affecting hospitals, emergency services, transportation, and other essential services. By implementing intrusion detection systems, security monitoring, and incident response plans, organizations can detect and respond to cyber threats in a timely manner, minimizing the potential impact on critical infrastructure and ensuring the continuity of essential services.

Safeguarding Industrial Control Systems (ICS): Many critical infrastructure systems rely on industrial control systems (ICS) to monitor and control physical processes. These systems, which include *SCADA (Supervisory Control and Data Acquisition)* and *DCS (Distributed*

Control Systems), are prime targets for cyberattacks. A successful breach in the **ICS** can enable attackers to manipulate or disrupt critical processes, leading to serious consequences. Implementing secure configurations, regular patch management, and strong access controls for ICS components are crucial for protecting critical infrastructure.

Threats to Public Safety: Cyberattacks targeting critical infrastructure can have direct implications for public safety. For instance, a cyberattack on transportation systems can compromise the safety of passengers, leading to accidents or disruptions in the movement of goods and people. By investing in cybersecurity measures, organizations can mitigate these threats, ensuring that critical infrastructure remains resilient and that public safety is not compromised.

Collaboration and Information Sharing: Protecting critical infrastructure requires collaboration and information sharing among stakeholders, including government agencies, industry sectors, and cybersecurity experts. Sharing threat intelligence, best practices, and incident response strategies can enhance the collective defense against cyber threats. Government entities can play a crucial role in facilitating such collaborations and establishing frameworks for information sharing to strengthen the overall cybersecurity posture of critical infrastructure.

Regulatory Compliance: Many countries have established regulations and standards that require organizations operating critical infrastructure to implement specific cybersecurity measures. Compliance with these regulations is essential not only to meet legal requirements but also to ensure the security and resilience of critical systems. Organizations must stay updated with relevant regulations, conduct regular security assessments, and implement necessary controls to achieve and maintain compliance.

Continuous Monitoring and Testing: Protecting critical infrastructure requires a proactive approach to cybersecurity. Continuous monitoring and testing of systems, networks, and applications are essential to identify vulnerabilities and potential security gaps. Regular security assessments, penetration testing, and vulnerability scanning help uncover weaknesses that could be exploited by cybercriminals. By promptly addressing these vulnerabilities, organizations can reduce the risk of successful cyberattacks on critical infrastructure.

Protecting critical infrastructure is a critical aspect of cybersecurity. Robust cybersecurity measures, collaboration among stakeholders, adherence to regulations, continuous monitoring, and testing are essential for safeguarding critical infrastructure from cyber threats. By prioritizing cybersecurity, organizations can ensure the resilience and reliability of critical systems, preserving public safety and maintaining the integrity of essential services.

Maintaining Trust and Confidence:

Cybersecurity plays a significant role in maintaining trust and confidence in the digital ecosystem. When individuals and businesses feel secure in their digital interactions, they are more likely to embrace technological advancements and engage in online activities. Effective cybersecurity measures build trust, foster collaboration, and encourage the responsible use of digital platforms.

Maintaining trust and confidence in the digital ecosystem is essential for individuals, businesses, and society as a whole.

Here's an elaboration on how cybersecurity helps achieve this objective:

Protecting Personal Information: Cybersecurity measures, such as encryption, secure authentication protocols, and robust data protection practices, are crucial for safeguarding personal information. When individuals feel confident that their personal data is protected, they are more likely to engage in online transactions, share information, and participate in digital platforms. By protecting personal information from unauthorized access, data breaches, and misuse, cybersecurity fosters trust and confidence in digital interactions.

Preventing Identity Theft and Fraud: Cybersecurity plays a crucial role in preventing identity theft and fraud, which are major concerns in the digital world. By implementing measures such as multi-factor authentication, secure payment gateways, and fraud detection systems, organizations can provide a secure environment for online transactions. This instills confidence in individuals, knowing that their financial transactions and personal information are protected from cybercriminals seeking to engage in fraudulent activities.

Building Customer Trust: Trust is a fundamental factor

in building strong customer relationships. When businesses prioritize cybersecurity and implement robust measures to protect customer data, it demonstrates a commitment to privacy and security. This, in turn, builds trust with customers, who feel confident that their information is handled responsibly. By consistently delivering secure and trustworthy digital experiences, businesses can establish a positive reputation, enhance customer loyalty, and gain a competitive edge.

Fostering Collaboration and Information Sharing: Trust is a vital component of collaboration and information sharing among individuals, businesses, and organizations. When there is confidence in the security and privacy of shared information, stakeholders are more willing to engage in collaborative efforts, share knowledge, and exchange ideas. Cybersecurity measures, such as secure communication channels, encrypted file sharing, and access controls, enable secure collaboration and promote a culture of trust and transparency.

Promoting Responsible Use of Digital Platforms: Cybersecurity helps promote the responsible use of digital platforms by establishing boundaries and guidelines for safe online behavior. By implementing content filtering, parental controls, and user awareness programs, individuals, particularly children and young adults, can navigate the digital landscape with confidence and security. Responsible use of digital platforms contributes to a positive and trustworthy online environment, fostering a sense of confidence in the digital ecosystem.

Enhancing Business Reputation and Competitiveness: Organizations that prioritize cybersecurity and demonstrate a strong commitment to protecting customer data and sensitive information tend to have a better reputation and competitive advantage. Customers and partners are more likely to trust and engage with businesses that invest in cybersecurity measures. This trust translates into increased customer loyalty, positive brand perception, and a competitive edge in the market.

Compliance with Regulatory Requirements: Cybersecurity is closely tied to regulatory requirements governing data protection and privacy. By complying with these regulations, organizations demonstrate their commitment to responsible data handling and maintaining a secure environment. Compliance with regulations such as the *General Data Protection Regulation (GDPR)* in the *European Union* or the *California Consumer Privacy Act*

(CCPA) helps build trust with customers and stakeholders, as it assures them that their rights and privacy are respected.

Cybersecurity is integral to maintaining trust and confidence in the digital ecosystem. By protecting personal information, preventing identity theft and fraud, building customer trust, fostering collaboration, promoting responsible use of digital platforms, enhancing business reputation, and ensuring compliance with regulations, cybersecurity establishes a foundation of trust that enables individuals and businesses to fully participate in the digital world with confidence and peace of mind.

Adapting to Technological Advancements:

As technology continues to evolve rapidly, so do cyber threats. Emerging technologies such as *artificial intelligence, internet of things (IoT),* and *cloud computing* bring numerous benefits, but they also introduce new vulnerabilities. Cybersecurity is essential for harnessing the potential of these technologies while mitigating associated risks. It ensures that innovation and adapting to Technological Advancements (continued): technological advancements can be embraced safely and securely, enabling organizations and individuals to leverage the benefits of emerging technologies without compromising their security and privacy.

As technology advances at a rapid pace, it brings both opportunities and challenges in terms of cybersecurity. Here's an elaboration on how cybersecurity adapts to technological advancements:

Artificial Intelligence (AI): AI offers immense potential for improving various aspects of cybersecurity. Machine learning algorithms can analyze vast amounts of data to detect patterns and anomalies, helping in threat detection and prevention. AI-powered security solutions can automate tasks, enhance incident response capabilities, and provide real-time insights into emerging threats. However, cybersecurity also needs to address the potential risks associated with AI, such as adversarial attacks or biases in AI algorithms.

Internet of Things (IoT): The proliferation of IoT devices introduces a multitude of endpoints and interconnected networks, expanding the attack surface for cyber threats. Cybersecurity in IoT focuses on securing devices, data, and communication protocols. It involves implementing strong authentication mechanisms, encryption protocols, and network segmentation to mitigate the risk of unauthorized access and data breaches. As IoT continues to evolve, cybersecurity measures must adapt to the unique challenges posed by interconnected devices.

Cloud Computing: Cloud computing offers scalability, flexibility, and cost-efficiency, but it also introduces security concerns. Cybersecurity in the cloud involves securing data at rest and in transit, implementing access controls, and ensuring compliance with data protection regulations. As organizations increasingly rely on cloud services, cybersecurity measures need to address the specific challenges of shared responsibility between cloud service providers and their customers, such as data privacy, identity and access management, and data segregation.

Mobile Security: With the widespread use of smartphones and mobile devices, mobile security has become paramount. Mobile cybersecurity focuses on securing mobile applications, preventing unauthorized access to devices, and protecting data transmitted over mobile networks. It includes measures such as mobile device management (MDM), mobile application security testing, and secure coding practices for app development. As mobile technology continues to advance, cybersecurity must adapt to the evolving threats and vulnerabilities in the mobile landscape.

Blockchain Technology: Blockchain technology, known for its decentralized and tamper-resistant nature, has gained attention in various industries. It offers potential applications in areas such as secure transactions, digital identity management, and supply chain transparency. Cybersecurity in blockchain focuses on securing the underlying technology, smart contracts, and ensuring the integrity and confidentiality of data stored on the blockchain. It involves identifying and addressing vulnerabilities in blockchain implementations and ensuring proper key management practices.

Quantum Computing: Quantum computing has the potential to break traditional cryptographic algorithms, which underpin many cybersecurity mechanisms. As quantum computing advances, cybersecurity needs to adapt by developing quantum-resistant encryption algorithms and security protocols. This includes researching and implementing post-quantum cryptography techniques to ensure that data remains secure even in the face of quantum attacks.

Cyber Threat Intelligence: Technological advancements also impact the nature of cyber threats. Cyber threat intelligence involves collecting, analyzing, and sharing information about emerging threats, attack techniques, and malicious actors. It utilizes technologies such as big data analytics, machine learning, and natural language processing to identify patterns and trends in cyber threats. By staying ahead of emerging threats, cybersecurity can proactively adapt its defenses and develop effective countermeasures.

Cybersecurity must continually adapt to technological advancements to effectively address evolving cyber threats. By leveraging emerging technologies such as AI, IoT, cloud computing, and blockchain, cybersecurity can enhance threat detection, incident response, and data protection. It must also anticipate and address the security challenges introduced by these advancements, ensuring the safe and secure adoption of new technologies without compromising privacy, integrity, and confidentiality. With a proactive and adaptive approach, cybersecurity can enable individuals and organizations to embrace technological advancements while mitigating associated risks.

Protecting Digital Reputation:

In today's digital landscape, reputation is everything. A single cybersecurity incident can have a significant impact on an individual's or organization's reputation. Data breaches, unauthorized access, or even a minor security incident can result in public scrutiny, loss of customer trust, and damage to brand reputation. By prioritizing cybersecurity, individuals and organizations can protect their digital reputation and maintain the trust of their stakeholders.

Protecting digital reputation is a crucial aspect of cybersecurity, as it directly impacts the trust and perception of individuals and organizations in the digital realm. Here's an elaboration on how cybersecurity safeguards digital reputation:

- **Preventing Data Breaches:** Data breaches can lead to the exposure of sensitive information, such as personal data, financial records, or intellectual property. By implementing robust cybersecurity measures, such as encryption, access controls, and network monitoring, individuals and organizations can significantly reduce the risk of data breaches. Proactive security measures help safeguard valuable information, ensuring that it remains confidential and protected from unauthorized access.

- **Safeguarding Online Presence:** An individual's or organization's online presence, including websites, social media accounts, and digital assets, needs to be protected from unauthorized alterations or malicious activities. Cybersecurity measures such as strong passwords, multi-factor authentication, and regular security updates help safeguard online platforms from hacking attempts, defacement, or unauthorized content modification. By securing their online presence, individuals and organizations can maintain control over their digital identity and reputation.

- **Mitigating Cyber Attacks:** Cyber attacks, such as distributed denial-of-service (DDoS) attacks or phishing attempts, can target an individual's or organization's online platforms, compromising their availability, integrity, and reputation. Implementing robust security measures, such as firewalls, intrusion detection systems, and security awareness training, helps mitigate the impact of cyber attacks. Proactive monitoring and incident response plans enable timely detection and response to potential threats, minimizing any negative impact on digital reputation.

- **Establishing Trust and Transparency:** Transparency plays a crucial role in building and maintaining trust in the digital space. Individuals and organizations should be transparent about their data collection and usage practices, providing clear privacy policies and consent mechanisms. By being transparent and accountable for their data handling practices, they can establish trust with their customers, users, or stakeholders. Regular communication about cybersecurity measures and initiatives also demonstrates a commitment to protecting digital assets and maintaining a strong reputation.

- **Engaging in Online Reputation Management:** Online reputation management involves actively monitoring and managing an individual's or organization's online presence and reputation. By using reputation management tools and services, individuals and organizations can monitor mentions, reviews, or comments related to their name or brand

and respond promptly to address any concerns or misinformation. This proactive approach allows them to maintain a positive digital reputation and promptly address any negative incidents or false information.

- **Prioritizing Cybersecurity Culture:** Cultivating a cybersecurity culture within an organization is crucial for protecting digital reputation. By educating employees about cybersecurity best practices, promoting responsible online behavior, and enforcing security policies, organizations can reduce the risk of insider threats and human error. Employees who are aware of cybersecurity risks and actively contribute to maintaining a secure environment can help safeguard digital reputation through their actions and awareness.

- **Monitoring and Responding to Online Threats**: It is essential to actively monitor online platforms, social media channels, and other digital spaces for potential threats or reputation-related incidents. By utilizing reputation monitoring tools or engaging professional services, individuals and organizations can proactively identify and respond to any negative online content, rumors, or malicious activities that could harm their digital reputation. Promptly addressing such incidents demonstrates a commitment to protecting one's reputation and minimizing the potential impact.

Cybersecurity plays a crucial role in protecting digital reputation. By preventing data breaches, safeguarding online presence, mitigating cyber attacks, establishing trust and transparency, engaging in online reputation management, prioritizing cybersecurity culture, and monitoring and responding to online threats, individuals and organizations can protect their digital reputation and maintain the trust and confidence of their stakeholders in the digital realm.

Safeguarding Data Integrity:

Data integrity is a critical aspect of cybersecurity. Cyber threats, such as data manipulation, unauthorized modifications, or ransomware attacks, can compromise the integrity of data, leading to severe consequences. Ensuring the integrity of data is essential for making informed decisions, maintaining accurate records, and preserving the trustworthiness of information.

Safeguarding data integrity is a fundamental aspect of cybersecurity that focuses on protecting the accuracy, consistency, and reliability of data throughout its lifecycle. Here's an elaboration on the importance of data integrity and how cybersecurity measures help safeguard it:

- **Trustworthy Decision-Making**: Data integrity ensures that the information used for decision-making is accurate, complete, and unaltered. When data is compromised or manipulated, it can lead to incorrect analyses, flawed conclusions, and poor decision-making. By implementing cybersecurity measures such as access controls, encryption, and audit trails, organizations can protect the integrity of their data, ensuring that it remains reliable and trustworthy.

- **Maintaining Accurate Records:** Data integrity is crucial for maintaining accurate records and preserving the historical information of individuals, organizations, or processes. Tampering with records can have severe legal and regulatory implications. By implementing mechanisms to verify data integrity, such as checksums or digital signatures, organizations can detect any unauthorized modifications to their records and ensure the accuracy and authenticity of their data.

- **Preserving Data Consistency:** Data integrity ensures that data remains consistent across different systems, databases, or platforms. Inconsistent data can lead to discrepancies, duplication, or conflicts that can impact operations, reporting, and analytics. Cybersecurity measures such as data validation checks, data synchronization protocols, and data governance frameworks help maintain data consistency and prevent inconsistencies that can arise due to unauthorized modifications or errors.

- **Detecting and Preventing Data Manipulation:** Cyber threats, such as data manipulation attacks, can alter data to misrepresent information, deceive stakeholders, or cause harm. Examples include unauthorized modifications of financial records, falsification of research data, or tampering with customer information. By implementing security controls, such as user access management, encryption, and data integrity monitoring tools, organizations can detect and prevent unauthorized data manipulation attempts, preserving the integrity of their data.

- **Protecting Against Ransomware:** Ransomware attacks encrypt data and hold it hostage until a ransom is paid. These attacks can disrupt business operations, compromise data integrity, and result in significant financial losses. Robust cybersecurity measures, including secure backups, network segmentation, and malware detection systems, help protect against ransomware attacks, ensuring the integrity and availability of data even in the event of an attack.

- **Ensuring Data Authenticity:** Data integrity ensures the authenticity of data, verifying that it comes from a trusted and reliable source. Cybersecurity measures such as digital certificates, cryptographic signatures, and secure communication protocols enable the authentication and verification of data sources. By ensuring data authenticity, organizations can trust the data they receive or exchange, mitigating the risk of relying on manipulated or falsified information.

- **Compliance with Regulatory Requirements:** Many industries and sectors have regulatory requirements that mandate the protection of data integrity. For example, in healthcare, patient records must remain accurate and unaltered to ensure patient safety and privacy. By implementing cybersecurity controls, organizations can demonstrate compliance with these regulations, protecting the integrity of sensitive data and avoiding legal and regulatory penalties.

Data integrity is a critical aspect of cybersecurity that ensures the accuracy, consistency, and reliability of data. By implementing cybersecurity measures such as access controls, encryption, data validation checks, and detection systems, organizations can safeguard data integrity, enabling trustworthy decision-making, maintaining accurate records, preserving data consistency, detecting and preventing data manipulation, protecting against ransomware, ensuring data authenticity, and complying with regulatory requirements.

Promoting Ethical and Responsible Technology Use:

Cybersecurity promotes ethical and responsible technology use by establishing guidelines and safeguards for the responsible handling of digital assets. It encourages individuals and organizations to consider the ethical implications of their actions in cyberspace, respect privacy rights, and protect sensitive information. By adhering to cybersecurity best practices, society can foster a culture of responsible technology use and digital citizenship.

Promoting ethical and responsible technology use is a crucial aspect of cybersecurity that goes beyond technical measures and addresses the broader societal impact of technology.

Here's an elaboration on the importance of promoting ethical and responsible technology use and how cybersecurity measures contribute to this goal:

- **Privacy Protection:** Cybersecurity plays a central role in protecting individuals' privacy rights. By implementing robust security measures, organizations can safeguard personal information, prevent unauthorized access, and ensure data confidentiality. Respecting privacy rights promotes ethical behavior by recognizing the importance of individuals' control over their personal data and fostering trust in digital interactions.

- **Data Ethics:** Cybersecurity encourages organizations and individuals to consider the ethical implications of data collection, storage, and usage. It promotes responsible data handling practices, such as data minimization (collecting only necessary data), purpose limitation (using data for specified purposes), and informed consent (obtaining consent before collecting or using personal data). Adhering to these principles helps protect individuals' privacy, prevent data misuse, and promote transparency and accountability.

- **Cyber Ethics Education:** Cybersecurity initiatives often include educational programs that promote cyber ethics and responsible technology use. These programs raise awareness about digital citizenship, online etiquette, and the ethical use of technology. By educating individuals from an early age about the potential risks, rights, and responsibilities associated with technology use, cybersecurity helps shape a generation of responsible digital citizens.

- **Ethical Hacking and Bug Bounty Programs:** Cybersecurity practices include ethical hacking and bug bounty programs, where skilled individuals are invited to test the security of systems and report vulnerabilities in a responsible manner. By creating platforms that reward ethical behavior, organizations encourage individuals to use their skills for positive purposes, uncover security flaws, and contribute to the overall improvement of cybersecurity.

- **Cybersecurity Policy and Governance:** Cybersecurity measures often involve the development and implementation of policies and governance frameworks that outline ethical guidelines for technology use. These policies address issues such as acceptable use of technology resources, responsible disclosure of vulnerabilities, and adherence to ethical standards in conducting cybersecurity activities. By establishing clear guidelines and expectations, organizations promote ethical behavior among employees and stakeholders.

- **Ethical AI and Algorithmic Transparency:** As artificial intelligence (AI) becomes more prevalent, cybersecurity plays a vital role in ensuring ethical AI practices. It involves addressing issues such as bias, fairness, and transparency in AI algorithms. Cybersecurity measures can help identify and mitigate bias in AI systems, promote transparency in algorithmic decision-making, and ensure that AI technologies are used in an ethical and responsible manner.

- **Responsible Information Sharing:** Cybersecurity encourages responsible information sharing within and across organizations, academic institutions, and government agencies. Sharing information about cybersecurity threats, vulnerabilities, and best practices enables collective defense and fosters a collaborative approach to addressing cybersecurity challenges. Responsible information sharing promotes ethical behavior by prioritizing the collective interest of protecting against cyber threats over individual interests.

Promoting ethical and responsible technology use is an integral part of cybersecurity. It involves protecting privacy rights, practicing responsible data handling, educating individuals about cyber ethics, encouraging ethical hacking and bug bounty programs, establishing cybersecurity policies and governance frameworks, addressing ethical concerns in AI, promoting responsible information sharing, and fostering a culture of digital citizenship. By integrating ethical considerations into cybersecurity practices, society can harness the benefits of technology while minimizing its negative impact and ensuring a more ethical and responsible digital future.

The importance of cybersecurity cannot be overstated in today's digital world. It encompasses the protection of personal information, safeguarding business operations, preserving national security, ensuring economic stability, mitigating cybercrime and fraud, preserving intellectual property, protecting critical infrastructure, maintaining trust and confidence, adapting to technological advancements, and promoting ethical technology use. By prioritizing cybersecurity, individuals, organizations, and governments can create a secure and resilient digital ecosystem, enabling innovation, growth, and trust in the digital age.

Consequences of Failing to Take Cybersecurity Seriously

Failing to take cybersecurity seriously can have severe consequences that can impact individuals, businesses, and even society as a whole. In an increasingly interconnected and digitized world, where cyber threats are becoming more sophisticated and prevalent, neglecting cybersecurity measures can lead to the following detrimental outcomes:

1. **Data Breaches:** One of the most immediate and damaging consequences of inadequate cybersecurity is the risk of data breaches. When organizations fail to implement robust security measures, they become vulnerable to cyberattacks that can result in the unauthorized access, theft, or exposure of sensitive information. This includes personal data, financial records, intellectual property, and trade secrets. Data breaches can lead to severe financial losses, reputational damage, and legal consequences, as organizations may be held liable for failing to protect confidential information.

2. **Financial Losses:** Cyberattacks can result in significant financial losses for individuals and organizations. The costs associated with responding to and recovering from a cyber incident can be substantial, including incident investigation, remediation efforts, legal fees, and potential regulatory fines. Moreover, organizations may suffer direct financial losses due to theft of funds, fraudulent activities, or disruption of critical business operations. Individuals may also experience financial losses through identity theft,

fraudulent transactions, or unauthorized access to their financial accounts.

3. **Reputational Damage:** A cybersecurity breach can severely damage an organization's reputation and erode customer trust. News of a data breach spreads quickly, leading to negative publicity and public scrutiny. Customers may lose confidence in the organization's ability to protect their information, resulting in a loss of business, decreased customer loyalty, and damaged brand reputation. Rebuilding trust and repairing a damaged reputation can be a lengthy and challenging process that impacts an organization's bottom line and long-term success.

4. **Legal and Regulatory Consequences:** Failing to prioritize cybersecurity can result in legal and regulatory consequences. Many jurisdictions have enacted data protection and privacy laws that impose obligations on organizations to protect personal information. In the event of a data breach, organizations may face investigations, fines, and lawsuits for non-compliance with these regulations. Additionally, industries that handle sensitive information, such as healthcare and financial

services, are subject to specific regulatory requirements, and non-compliance can lead to severe penalties and sanctions.

5. **Operational Disruption:** Cyberattacks can disrupt business operations, leading to significant downtime, loss of productivity, and impaired service delivery. Ransomware attacks, for example, can encrypt critical data and systems, rendering them inaccessible until a ransom is paid. This can result in substantial financial losses and disruptions to essential services. Additionally, organizations may incur additional costs in restoring systems, conducting forensic investigations, and implementing measures to prevent future incidents.

6. **Intellectual Property Theft:** Businesses that fail to protect their intellectual property (IP) may face the theft or unauthorized use of valuable trade secrets, patents, copyrights, and proprietary information. This can result in significant financial losses, as competitors gain access to confidential research and development efforts or exploit innovative ideas without authorization. Intellectual property theft can undermine a company's competitive advantage,

hinder future innovation, and damage its market position.

7. **Societal Impact:** The consequences of inadequate cybersecurity go beyond individual organizations and can have a broader societal impact. Cyberattacks targeting critical infrastructure, government institutions, or healthcare systems can disrupt essential services, compromise public safety, and undermine national security. Such incidents can have far-reaching consequences on public trust, economic stability, and social well-being.

Failing to take cybersecurity seriously can result in data breaches, financial losses, reputational damage, legal and regulatory consequences, operational disruptions, intellectual property theft, and broader societal impacts. It is crucial for individuals and organizations to prioritize cybersecurity measures to protect sensitive information, preserve trust, and mitigate the potentially devastating consequences of cyber threats. By investing in robust cybersecurity practices, organizations can reduce the risk of cyber incidents, protect their assets, and maintain their competitive edge.

Summary

Real-world examples and case studies provide valuable insights into the impact of cybersecurity incidents and the importance of robust security measures. By studying past incidents and their consequences, individuals and organizations can gain a deeper understanding of the potential risks they face and learn from the mistakes of others. Real-world examples highlight the need for proactive cybersecurity measures, preparedness, and swift incident response.

Action Points

1. **Case Study Analysis:** Conduct case study analyses of notable cybersecurity incidents to understand the tactics, techniques, and vulnerabilities exploited by attackers. Identify the weaknesses in security practices that allowed the incidents to occur and explore the potential consequences. Use these insights to strengthen existing security measures and develop preventive strategies.

2. **Incident Response Planning:** Develop and implement comprehensive incident response plans

based on real-world case studies. Consider various scenarios and create protocols for detecting, responding to, and recovering from cybersecurity incidents. Test and update these plans regularly to ensure they remain effective and aligned with emerging threats.

3. **Industry-Specific Case Studies:** Study case studies relevant to your specific industry or sector to understand the unique cybersecurity challenges and vulnerabilities faced by organizations in that domain. Identify common attack vectors, compliance requirements, and best practices specific to your industry. Use this knowledge to tailor security strategies and controls accordingly.

4. **Collaboration and Information Sharing:** Participate in industry-specific forums, information-sharing platforms, and cybersecurity communities to learn from real-world experiences shared by other organizations. Engage in open discussions, exchange knowledge, and share best practices to collectively strengthen cybersecurity measures and build a resilient community.

5. **Learn from Success Stories:** Alongside studying

cybersecurity incidents, also examine success stories and examples of organizations effectively mitigating cyber threats. Identify the strategies, technologies, and practices that contributed to their successful defense against attacks. Implement similar approaches in your own security framework to bolster resilience.

Chapter 5

Practical Tools and Resources - Recommended Software and Online Resources

When it comes to software and online resources for various purposes, there is a wide range of options available to individuals and organizations.

Here, we will explore some recommended software and online resources across different categories:

Cybersecurity Tools:

Antivirus and Antimalware Software: Popular antivirus solutions like *Norton, McAfee, and Bitdefender* offer comprehensive protection against viruses, malware, and other online threats.

Firewalls: Software firewalls like *Windows Firewall and ZoneAlarm* help monitor and control incoming and outgoing network traffic to protect against unauthorized access.

Password Managers: Tools like *LastPass, Dashlane, and 1Password* securely store and generate strong passwords, ensuring better password management and reducing the risk of password-related vulnerabilities.

Virtual Private Networks (VPNs): VPN services such as *NordVPN, ExpressVPN, and CyberGhost* encrypt internet connections, enhancing online privacy and security.

Virtual Private Networks (VPNs) are essential cybersecurity tools that provide a secure and private connection over public networks. They encrypt data transmitted between your device and the internet, preventing unauthorized access and eavesdropping. VPNs create a secure tunnel that masks your IP address and encrypts your online activities, making it difficult for cybercriminals, internet service providers, or government agencies to monitor or track your online behavior.

When you use a VPN, your data is encrypted and routed through a server located in a different geographic location. This allows you to bypass geographical restrictions and access region-restricted content, such as streaming services or websites blocked in your location. It also protects your privacy by masking your real IP address and making it appear as if you are accessing the internet from the location of the VPN server.

VPNs are particularly useful when connecting to public Wi-Fi networks, such as those found in cafes, airports, or hotels. These networks are often unsecured, making it easy for cybercriminals to intercept data transmitted over them. By using a VPN, your data is encrypted, ensuring that even if someone tries to intercept your communications, they won't be able to decipher the information.

Moreover, VPNs are valuable tools for remote workers or individuals accessing corporate networks. They provide a secure connection between remote devices and the company's internal network, allowing employees to access sensitive information and resources securely. This protects the confidentiality and integrity of corporate data, even when employees are working from outside the office.

It's important to choose a reputable VPN provider that prioritizes security, privacy, and transparency. Look for VPNs that have a strict no-logs policy, meaning they do not store any records of your online activities. Additionally, consider the encryption protocols and strength offered by the VPN, as well as the number and locations of their server network.

While VPNs offer significant benefits, it's worth noting that they may introduce some performance overhead due to the encryption and rerouting of data. However, the trade-off in terms of security and privacy is well worth it, especially when using the internet in potentially risky environments.

VPNs are powerful tools for enhancing online security and privacy. They encrypt your data, protect your identity, and allow you to access the internet more securely, regardless of your location. By using a VPN, you can safeguard your sensitive information, browse the web anonymously, and ensure your online activities remain private and protected.

Productivity and Collaboration Tools:

Productivity and collaboration tools have become essential in today's digital work environment, enabling individuals and teams to work efficiently, communicate effectively, and collaborate seamlessly.

Here are some popular productivity and collaboration tools:

Office Suites: *Microsoft Office, Google Workspace, and LibreOffice* are comprehensive productivity suites that include word processing, spreadsheet, and presentation software. These tools provide essential features for creating, editing, and formatting documents, spreadsheets, and presentations, making them indispensable for various professional tasks.

Project Management Tools: *Trello, Asana, and Jira* are project management tools that help teams organize and manage tasks, track progress, and facilitate collaboration. These tools provide a visual interface for creating and assigning tasks, setting deadlines, and tracking the status of projects. They also offer features like task dependencies, file attachments, and comment sections, allowing teams to work together efficiently and stay organized.

Communication and Collaboration: Communication and collaboration tools like *Slack, Microsoft Teams, and Zoom* have become essential for remote work and virtual collaboration. These tools provide instant messaging, video conferencing, and file sharing capabilities, allowing team members to communicate in real-time, share information, and collaborate on projects. They also offer features like channels or chat groups, screen sharing, and integrations with other tools, enhancing teamwork and collaboration.

In addition to these tools, there are many other productivity and collaboration solutions available, each with its own unique features and capabilities. It's important to choose tools that align with your specific needs and the requirements of your team or organization. Consider factors such as *ease of use, scalability, integrations with other systems, and security features* when selecting productivity and collaboration tools.

By leveraging these tools effectively, individuals and teams can enhance their productivity, streamline workflows, and improve collaboration. They provide a centralized platform for communication, task management, and document collaboration, reducing the need for multiple tools and inefficient workflows. With real-time collaboration features, remote team members can work together seamlessly, irrespective of their physical locations.

However, it's crucial to ensure the security and privacy of the data shared and stored within these tools. Familiarize yourself with the security features offered by each tool, such as data encryption, access controls, and user authentication.

Additionally, regularly update the software and follow best practices for password management and data protection to mitigate potential risks.

Productivity and collaboration tools are essential for modern work environments, enabling individuals and teams to work more efficiently, communicate effectively, and collaborate seamlessly. By leveraging these tools, organizations can streamline their workflows, improve productivity, and enhance collaboration, ultimately leading to better outcomes and increased success.

Online Learning Platforms:

Online learning platforms have revolutionized the way people acquire knowledge and develop new skills. With advancements in technology, access to educational resources and expert instruction is no longer limited to traditional classrooms. Here are some popular online learning platforms and their key features:

Massive Open Online Courses (MOOCs): Platforms such as *Coursera, Udemy, and edX* offer a wide range of online courses taught by leading institutions and professionals from around the world. These courses cover diverse subjects, including computer science, business, humanities, and more. **MOOCs** provide flexibility in terms of scheduling and pacing, allowing learners to access course materials and complete assignments at their own convenience.

Technical and Programming Resources: Websites like *Stack Overflow, GitHub, and W3Schools* serve as valuable resources for programmers and developers. **Stack Overflow**, in particular, is a popular platform where developers can ask questions, find answers, and engage in discussions related to coding and software development. **GitHub** provides a platform for collaborative coding, version control, and sharing open-source projects. **W3Schools** offers comprehensive tutorials and references for web development languages such as *HTML, CSS, JavaScript, and more.*

Language Learning: Language learning platforms such as *Duolingo, Babbel, and Rosetta Stone* offer interactive courses for individuals interested in acquiring new language skills. These platforms provide a variety of exercises, quizzes, and games to engage learners in a fun and interactive way. Users can learn at their own pace, track their progress, and receive instant feedback on their language proficiency.

These online learning platforms provide several advantages.

First, they offer flexibility and convenience, allowing learners to access educational resources anytime, anywhere, and at their own pace. This is particularly beneficial for individuals with busy schedules or those who prefer self-paced learning.

Second, these platforms often offer a wide range of courses, enabling learners to explore diverse subjects and acquire specialized skills.

Third, the interactive nature of online learning platforms enhances engagement and retention, as learners can actively participate in exercises, quizzes, and discussions.

However, it is important to note that online learning platforms vary in terms of course quality, instructor expertise, and certification. It is advisable to research and read reviews before enrolling in a course.

Additionally, learners should consider their own learning preferences and goals to select courses that align with their needs.

Online learning platforms provide a wealth of educational resources, courses, and opportunities for individuals to expand their knowledge and skills. Whether you are interested in professional development, technical skills, language learning, or personal enrichment, these platforms offer a convenient and accessible avenue for acquiring new knowledge and advancing your learning journey. By leveraging these online learning platforms effectively, individuals can gain valuable skills, enhance their career prospects, and foster a lifelong love for learning.

Design and Creative Tools:

Design and creative tools have empowered individuals and businesses to express their creativity and bring their ideas to life. Whether you are a graphic designer, video editor, or website developer, there are various software and platforms available to support your creative endeavors. Here are some popular design and creative tools:

Graphic Design: *Adobe Photoshop and Illustrator* are industry-leading software applications for graphic design. They provide a wide range of tools and features for creating stunning visuals, including logos, illustrations, and marketing materials. **Canva** is another popular choice, offering a user-friendly interface and a vast library of pre-designed templates that allow even non-designers to create professional-looking graphics.

Video Editing: When it comes to video editing, professionals often turn to software like *Adobe Premiere Pro, Final Cut Pro, and DaVinci Resolve*. These tools offer advanced features for editing, color grading, and visual effects, enabling users to produce high-quality videos for various purposes, including films, advertisements, and online content.

Website Development: *Content management systems (CMS)* like **WordPress** have made website development more accessible to individuals with limited technical knowledge. With a wide range of themes, plugins, and customization options, WordPress allows users to create and manage websites with ease. Additionally, website builders like *Wix and Squarespace* offer drag-and-drop interfaces and pre-designed templates, making it simple for beginners to build professional-looking websites without coding.

These design and creative tools provide numerous benefits. They empower individuals to unleash their creativity, enhance their visual communication skills, and effectively convey their message to their target audience. With these tools, professionals and enthusiasts alike can create visually appealing designs, engaging videos, and interactive websites.

Moreover, these tools often come with extensive resources, including tutorials, forums, and online communities, which can help users learn and improve their skills. The availability of templates, stock images, and other design assets also accelerates the creative process and enables users to achieve professional results without starting from scratch.

It is worth noting that while these tools offer powerful features and capabilities, they may also have learning curves, especially for beginners. *It is recommended to take advantage of tutorials, online courses, and other learning resources to fully harness the potential of these tools.*

Design and creative tools have transformed the way individuals and businesses approach graphic design, video editing, and website development. Whether you are a professional designer or someone looking to unleash their creativity, these tools provide the necessary resources and functionalities to bring ideas to life. By leveraging these tools effectively, individuals can create visually captivating designs, compelling videos, and engaging websites that leave a lasting impact on their audience.

Cloud Storage and File Sharing:

Cloud storage and file sharing tools have revolutionized

the way we store, access, and share our digital files. They offer convenient and secure solutions for managing files across multiple devices and collaborating with others. Here are some popular cloud storage and file sharing tools:

Cloud Storage Providers: *Google Drive, Dropbox, and OneDrive* are among the leading cloud storage providers. These platforms offer generous storage space and allow users to store files and folders in the cloud. They provide seamless synchronization across devices, enabling users to access their files from anywhere with an internet connection. With robust security measures in place, including encryption and multi-factor authentication, these services ensure the privacy and integrity of stored data.

File Transfer and Sharing: When it comes to transferring large files or sharing documents with others, tools like *WeTransfer, Send Anywhere, and ShareFile* come in handy. These platforms allow users to upload files and generate shareable links that can be sent to recipients. With simple and intuitive interfaces, these tools streamline the file-sharing process, eliminating the need for cumbersome email attachments or physical storage devices.

Using cloud storage and file sharing tools offers several advantages.

Firstly, they provide flexibility and accessibility, as files can be accessed and edited from different devices, making collaboration more efficient. Users can easily share files with colleagues, clients, or friends, granting them the ability to view, comment, or edit documents in real-time.

Secondly, cloud storage ensures data redundancy and protection against hardware failures or accidents. Files stored in the cloud are backed up and stored on remote servers, reducing the risk of data loss. This feature is particularly valuable for businesses or individuals with critical data that needs to be preserved.

Thirdly, these tools enhance productivity by eliminating the need for physical storage devices and allowing for seamless file synchronization. Users can access their files on the go, making it easier to work remotely or collaborate with team members from different locations.

While cloud storage and file sharing tools offer convenience and efficiency, it is essential to consider security and privacy. Users should opt for reputable service providers that employ robust encryption methods and provide options for securing files and controlling access permissions. Additionally, it is advisable to use strong, unique passwords and enable two-factor authentication to further enhance the security of cloud storage accounts.

Cloud storage and file sharing tools have transformed the way we store, access, and share our digital files. They provide convenient and secure solutions for managing files across multiple devices, enabling seamless collaboration and enhancing productivity. By leveraging these tools effectively, individuals and businesses can ensure data accessibility, improve workflow efficiency, and simplify the process of sharing files with others.

Online Security Resources:

Online security resources play a crucial role in keeping individuals and organizations informed about the latest cybersecurity threats, best practices, and guidelines. Here are some valuable online resources in the field of cybersecurity:

Cybersecurity Organizations: *Cybersecurity and Infrastructure Security Agency (CISA), National Institute of Standards and Technology (NIST), and Information*

Systems Security Association (ISSA) are prominent organizations that provide comprehensive resources and guidance on cybersecurity. Their websites offer access to white papers, reports, frameworks, and guidelines that can help individuals and businesses enhance their cybersecurity posture. These organizations also conduct training programs and workshops to promote cybersecurity awareness and education.

Security Blogs and News: Websites like *KrebsOnSecurity, Dark Reading, and The Hacker News* are dedicated to covering the latest news, analysis, and insights on cybersecurity. These blogs provide a wealth of information on emerging threats, data breaches, vulnerabilities, and industry trends. They often feature in-depth articles, interviews with cybersecurity experts, and practical advice for individuals and organizations to improve their security practices. Subscribing to these blogs or following them on social media can help users stay updated on the evolving landscape of cybersecurity.

Vendor and Industry Websites: Many cybersecurity software and service providers maintain informative websites with resources and educational materials. Companies like *Symantec, McAfee, and Palo Alto*

Networks provide security blogs, white papers, webinars, and case studies that offer insights into various aspects of cybersecurity. These resources can help users understand different threats, evaluate security solutions, and implement effective cybersecurity strategies.

Online Forums and Communities: Online forums and communities dedicated to cybersecurity serve as platforms for professionals and enthusiasts to share knowledge, seek advice, and engage in discussions. Platforms like *Reddit's r/netsec, Stack Exchange Security, and the ISC SANS* Community provide spaces where users can ask questions, share experiences, and learn from the expertise of others in the field. Participating in these communities can offer valuable insights, practical tips, and real-world experiences related to cybersecurity.

Government Websites and Initiatives: Many government agencies and departments have dedicated sections on their websites that focus on cybersecurity. These websites offer resources, guidelines, and best practices tailored to specific industries and user groups. Examples include the *Federal Trade Commission's (FTC) cybersecurity resources for consumers and businesses, the Department of Homeland Security's (DHS)*

Stop.Think.Connect campaign, and the European Union Agency for Cybersecurity (ENISA) website. These resources provide valuable information on cybersecurity threats, privacy, online safety, and protection against cybercrime.

By leveraging these online security resources, individuals and organizations can access valuable information, stay updated on the latest threats, and gain insights into best practices for securing their digital assets. It is important to regularly visit these resources, follow industry news, and engage with the cybersecurity community to foster a proactive and informed approach to cybersecurity.

Open-Source Software:

Open-source software refers to software that is freely available, allowing users to access, use, modify, and distribute the source code. It is developed collaboratively by a community of developers, who contribute their expertise and code improvements to create robust and innovative solutions. Open-source software has gained significant popularity and has become a vital component of the technology landscape. Here are some key points about open-source software:

Accessibility and Cost: One of the major advantages of open-source software is its accessibility. Users can download and use open-source software without any licensing costs. This makes it an attractive option for individuals, small businesses, educational institutions, and nonprofit organizations with limited budgets. It allows users to access high-quality software solutions without the financial burden associated with proprietary software.

Transparency and Security: Open-source software promotes transparency by making the source code openly available. This enables users to inspect, review, and verify the code for security vulnerabilities, bugs, or malicious intent. The collaborative nature of open-source development encourages peer review and auditing, which can result in more secure software. Furthermore, the active community of developers can quickly identify and fix security issues, ensuring prompt updates and patches.

Customizability and Flexibility: Open-source software provides users with the freedom to modify and customize the software according to their specific needs. The availability of the source code allows developers to adapt the software to fit their requirements, add new features, or integrate it with other systems. This flexibility empowers users to tailor the software to their unique workflows and achieve greater efficiency and productivity.

Innovation and Collaboration: Open-source software thrives on collaboration and encourages innovation. The open nature of the development process enables a global community of developers to contribute their expertise, ideas, and improvements to the software. This collaborative effort often results in rapid innovation, as developers can build upon each other's work and leverage the collective knowledge and skills of the community. This dynamic ecosystem fosters continuous improvement and the evolution of the software over time.

Wide Range of Applications: Open-source software spans various domains and serves a wide range of applications. From operating systems *(e.g., Linux) and web servers (e.g., Apache) to databases (e.g., MySQL) and media players (e.g., VLC),* open-source software covers diverse areas of technology. Additionally, there are open-source solutions available for web development, content management systems, office productivity, graphics editing, data analysis, and much more. The versatility of open-source software allows users to find suitable tools for their specific needs.

Community Support: Open-source software typically has a vibrant community of users and developers who provide support and guidance. Online forums, mailing lists, documentation, and user communities play a vital role in helping users troubleshoot issues, find solutions, and exchange knowledge. The community support ensures that users are not alone in their journey with open-source software and can tap into the collective wisdom of the community when facing challenges.

It is important to note that while open-source software offers numerous benefits, it also requires careful consideration. Users should evaluate the software's stability, community support, and compatibility with their specific requirements before adoption. Additionally, organizations should ensure proper implementation, configuration, and ongoing maintenance of open-source software to maximize its benefits and mitigate any potential risks.

Overall, open-source software has revolutionized the technology industry by providing accessible, customizable, and secure solutions. It empowers individuals, businesses, and communities to leverage high-quality software without the restrictions of proprietary licensing, fostering collaboration, innovation, and technological advancement. It is important to note that while these software and online resources are widely recognized and recommended, individual needs and preferences may vary. It is advisable to research and evaluate options based on specific requirements and read user reviews before selecting the most suitable software or online resource for a particular purpose.

Summary

Practical tools and resources play a vital role in cybersecurity, providing individuals and organizations with the means to enhance their security measures and mitigate cyber risks. These tools encompass a wide range of categories, including antivirus software, firewalls, password managers, virtual private networks (VPNs), productivity and collaboration tools, online learning platforms, design and creative tools, cloud storage and file sharing services, online security resources, and open-source software. By leveraging these tools and resources, users can proactively address cybersecurity challenges, protect their digital assets, and foster a secure digital environment.

Action Points

1. **Assess Your Needs:** Begin by evaluating your cybersecurity needs and identifying the specific tools and resources that align with your requirements. Consider factors such as the size of your organization, the nature of your digital activities, and the level of security you aim to achieve. This assessment will help you prioritize the tools and resources that are most relevant to your situation.

2. **Research and Evaluate:** Conduct thorough research to identify the most reputable and effective tools and resources in the cybersecurity landscape. Consider factors such as user reviews, industry recognition, features, reliability, and compatibility with your existing systems. Evaluate multiple options within each category to ensure you select the most suitable solutions for your cybersecurity needs.

3. **Implement a Layered Approach:** Recognize that no single tool or resource can provide complete protection against cyber threats. Adopt a layered approach to cybersecurity by combining multiple tools and resources to create a comprehensive defense strategy. Implement a mix of preventive, detective, and responsive measures to enhance your overall security posture.

4. **Stay Informed and Updated:** Cyber threats are continually evolving, so it is essential to stay informed about the latest trends, vulnerabilities, and best practices in cybersecurity. Regularly access online security resources, follow reputable cybersecurity blogs and news outlets, and participate in relevant forums or communities to stay up to date. This information will help you make informed decisions when selecting and utilizing cybersecurity tools and resources.

5. **Continuously Monitor and Improve:** Cybersecurity is an ongoing process that requires constant monitoring and improvement. Regularly assess the effectiveness of your chosen tools and resources, review their performance, and identify

areas for enhancement. Stay proactive by regularly updating software, implementing patches, and ensuring that your tools and resources align with emerging threats and evolving cybersecurity standards.

Chapter 6

Privacy in The Digital Age - The Growing Concern of Privacy in the Digital Age

In the digital age, the growing concern of privacy has become a prominent issue. Rapid advancements in technology, the widespread use of the internet, and the exponential growth of data collection and sharing have raised significant questions about the protection of personal information and individual privacy. This section will explore the various aspects and implications of privacy in the digital age.

1. **Data Collection and Surveillance:** With the proliferation of online services, social media platforms, and mobile applications, individuals are continuously generating and sharing vast amounts of personal data. This data includes browsing history, location information, communication logs, preferences, and even biometric data. Governments, corporations, and other entities are collecting and analyzing this data for various purposes, including

targeted advertising, behavioral analysis, and surveillance. The extent and sophistication of data collection have raised concerns about the erosion of privacy and the potential for misuse or abuse of personal information.

2. **Online Tracking and Profiling:** Online tracking techniques, such as cookies, device fingerprinting, and tracking pixels, are commonly used to monitor individuals' online activities. These techniques enable the creation of detailed profiles that capture individuals' preferences, interests, and behavior. Such profiles are often used for personalized marketing, content delivery, and recommendation systems. However, the extensive tracking and profiling raise concerns about individuals' autonomy and the potential manipulation of their choices and decisions. Additionally, the aggregation of data from multiple sources can result in the creation of comprehensive and intrusive profiles, further compromising privacy.

3. **Cybersecurity and Data Breaches:** The frequency and scale of data breaches have increased

significantly in recent years. Cybercriminals target organizations to gain unauthorized access to sensitive data, including personal information, financial records, and intellectual property. Data breaches not only expose individuals to identity theft and fraud but also erode trust in organizations' ability to protect personal data. The consequences of data breaches can be long-lasting and far-reaching, resulting in financial losses, reputational damage, and emotional distress for those affected.

4. **Government Surveillance and Mass Surveillance:** Governments around the world engage in various forms of surveillance to ensure national security, investigate criminal activities, and combat terrorism. However, the extent of government surveillance, particularly mass surveillance programs, has sparked debates about the balance between security and privacy. Mass surveillance involves the indiscriminate collection of data from a broad range of individuals, often without their knowledge or consent. Concerns have been raised regarding the potential infringement of civil liberties, the chilling

effect on free speech and dissent, and the erosion of trust in government institutions.

5. **Consent and Lack of Control:** In the digital age, individuals often face challenges in understanding and managing their consent regarding the collection, use, and sharing of their personal data. Privacy policies and terms of service agreements are often complex, lengthy, and filled with legal jargon, making it difficult for individuals to make informed decisions about their privacy rights. Additionally, individuals have limited control over their personal information once it is shared with third parties, and it can be challenging to track or revoke consent.

6. **Reputational Risks and Discrimination:** The availability and persistence of digital information have significant implications for individuals' reputations. Online content, including social media posts, comments, and photographs, can be easily accessed, shared, and used to make judgments or decisions about individuals. Inappropriate or damaging information, whether true or false, can have long-lasting consequences, including

reputation damage, social stigma, and even discrimination in areas such as employment, housing, or financial services.

7. **Ethical Considerations:** The ethical implications of privacy in the digital age are also of great concern. Questions arise regarding the ethical collection and use of personal data, transparency in data practices, and the potential for discrimination or bias in algorithmic decision-making. Ethical frameworks such as informed consent, purpose limitation, data minimization, and data anonymization are crucial in addressing these concerns and ensuring that privacy rights are respected.

8. **Global Privacy Regulations**: In response to the growing concerns about privacy in the digital age, governments and regulatory bodies have implemented various privacy laws and regulations. Examples include the *General Data Protection Regulation (GDPR)* in the European Union, the *California Consumer Privacy Act (CCPA)* in the United States, and the *Personal Information Protection and Electronic Documents Act (PIPEDA)*

in Canada. These regulations aim to enhance individuals' rights, provide transparency in data practices, and impose obligations on organizations to protect personal data. Compliance with these regulations is essential for organizations to demonstrate their commitment to privacy and avoid legal consequences.

9. **Privacy-enhancing Technologies:** To address privacy concerns, there is a growing focus on developing and implementing *privacy-enhancing technologies (PETs)*. **PETs** aim to protect individuals' privacy by incorporating privacy features into the design of software, systems, and services. Examples include secure communication protocols, anonymization techniques, differential privacy, and decentralized identity systems. These technologies help individuals maintain control over their personal data and mitigate privacy risks.

10. **Individual Privacy Empowerment:** In the face of growing privacy concerns, individuals are becoming more aware of the importance of protecting their privacy and are taking steps to assert their rights.

Privacy-conscious individuals are adopting privacy-enhancing tools, such as *virtual private networks (VPNs)*, encrypted messaging apps, and ad-blockers, to safeguard their online activities. Privacy advocacy groups and organizations are also working to educate the public, raise awareness about privacy risks, and advocate for stronger privacy protections.

The growing concern of privacy in the digital age is a multifaceted issue that encompasses data collection and surveillance, online tracking and profiling, cybersecurity and data breaches, government surveillance, consent and lack of control, reputational risks, ethical considerations, privacy regulations, privacy-enhancing technologies, and individual privacy empowerment. It is crucial for individuals, organizations, governments, and regulatory bodies to collaborate in addressing these concerns, striking a balance between privacy and other societal needs, and ensuring that privacy rights are protected in the digital era.

Protecting Personal Information Online

In the digital age, where personal information is constantly collected, shared, and stored online, it is essential to prioritize the protection of personal information. Safeguarding personal data helps prevent identity theft, financial fraud, reputational damage, and other malicious activities. Here are key strategies and best practices for protecting personal information online:

1. **Use Strong and Unique Passwords:** Creating strong and unique passwords is the first line of defense in protecting personal information. Use a combination of uppercase and lowercase letters, numbers, and special characters. Avoid using easily guessable passwords like birthdays or common phrases. Consider using password managers to generate and store complex passwords securely.

2. **Enable Two-Factor Authentication (2FA):** Two-factor authentication adds an extra layer of security to online accounts. It requires users to provide a second form of verification, such as a unique code sent to a mobile device, in addition to a password. Enable 2FA whenever available, especially for critical accounts like email, banking, and social media.

3. **Be Cautious of Phishing Attempts:** Phishing is a common tactic used by cybercriminals to trick individuals into revealing personal information. Be vigilant of suspicious emails, messages, or calls that request sensitive data or urge immediate action. Avoid clicking on links or downloading attachments from unknown sources. Verify the legitimacy of requests by contacting the organization directly.

4. **Secure Wi-Fi Networks:** When using public Wi-Fi networks, exercise caution to protect personal information. Avoid accessing sensitive accounts or sharing confidential data when connected to unsecured Wi-Fi. Instead, use virtual private networks (VPNs) to encrypt internet traffic and establish a secure connection.

5. **Regularly Update Software and Devices:** Keep software, operating systems, and apps up to date. Regularly install security patches and updates to protect against known vulnerabilities. Enable automatic updates whenever possible to ensure ongoing protection.

6. **Be Mindful of Social Media Sharing:** Limit the amount of personal information shared on social media platforms. Adjust privacy settings to control who can access your posts, photos, and personal details. Avoid sharing sensitive information, such as your full address, phone number, or financial details, publicly.

7. **Review Privacy Policies and Terms of Service:** When signing up for online services, read and understand the privacy policies and terms of service. Pay attention to how your data will be collected, used, and shared. Be cautious of services that require excessive data sharing or have questionable privacy practices.

8. **Secure Data Storage and Backup:** Protect personal information stored on devices and in cloud services. Use strong encryption for sensitive files and consider storing them in encrypted containers or password-protected folders. Regularly back up important data to ensure it can be recovered in case of data loss or device theft.

9. **Be Selective with Online Forms and Requests:** Exercise caution when filling out online forms or providing personal information. Only provide necessary details and avoid sharing sensitive information unless it is necessary for a trusted purpose. Verify the credibility and security measures of websites before submitting personal data.

10. **Educate Yourself:** Stay informed about the latest cybersecurity threats, scams, and best practices for protecting personal information online. Educate yourself about common attack techniques like phishing, malware, and social engineering. By staying informed, you can better protect yourself and make informed decisions regarding your online privacy.

Remember, protecting personal information online requires a proactive and mindful approach. By implementing these strategies and adopting good cybersecurity habits, individuals can significantly reduce the risk of their personal information being compromised. It is essential to prioritize privacy and take the necessary steps to safeguard personal data in the digital realm.

Advocating for Stronger Privacy Protections

In the digital age, where personal data is constantly collected, analyzed, and shared, advocating for stronger privacy protections has become crucial. Privacy is a fundamental right that ensures individuals have control over their personal information and are protected from unwarranted surveillance, data breaches, and misuse of their data. Advocating for stronger privacy protections involves raising awareness, promoting legislative changes, and fostering a culture of privacy-conscious behavior. Here are key areas to focus on when advocating for stronger privacy protections:

1. **Education and Awareness:** Increasing public awareness about privacy issues is an essential first step in advocating for stronger privacy protections. Educate individuals about their rights and the importance of protecting their personal data. Promote the understanding of privacy-related risks, such as identity theft, data breaches, and intrusive surveillance, and their potential consequences.

Encourage individuals to adopt privacy-conscious behavior in their daily lives.

2. **Encouraging Privacy by Design:** Advocate for the integration of privacy by design principles into the development of products, services, and systems. Privacy by design entails embedding privacy features and considerations at the early stages of design and development, ensuring privacy is a core aspect of any technological solution. Encourage organizations to adopt privacy-enhancing technologies, data minimization practices, and privacy impact assessments to prioritize privacy throughout the entire lifecycle of a product or service.

3. **Strengthening Privacy Laws and Regulations:** Advocate for the enactment and strengthening of privacy laws and regulations that protect individuals' personal information. Support legislative efforts that enhance data protection, promote transparency, and establish clear guidelines for data collection, storage, and use. Advocate for laws that give individuals greater control over their personal data, including the right to access, correct, and delete their information.

Push for robust enforcement mechanisms and significant penalties for privacy violations.

4. **Enhanced Data Breach Notification:** Advocate for mandatory data breach notification laws that require organizations to notify individuals in a timely manner when a data breach occurs. Encourage stricter requirements for organizations to disclose breaches and provide accurate and transparent information about the scope and impact of the breach. Push for measures that hold organizations accountable for safeguarding personal data and prompt action to mitigate the consequences of breaches.

5. **Balancing National Security and Privacy:** Advocate for the development of policies and practices that strike a balance between national security interests and individual privacy rights. Encourage governments to adopt surveillance oversight mechanisms, judicial authorization for intrusive surveillance measures, and regular transparency reports on surveillance activities. Advocate for the protection of encryption as a

critical tool for securing individuals' privacy while maintaining a strong stance against unlawful activities.

6. **Privacy in Emerging Technologies:** Advocate for privacy protections in emerging technologies such as artificial intelligence, internet of things (IoT), and biometrics. Encourage the development of ethical guidelines and standards that prioritize privacy considerations in the design, deployment, and use of these technologies. Advocate for clear consent mechanisms, data protection, and privacy safeguards that align with the evolving technological landscape.

7. **Collaboration and Partnerships:** Collaborate with like-minded organizations, privacy advocates, and industry stakeholders to amplify the voice for stronger privacy protections. Join forces with consumer advocacy groups, civil liberties organizations, and academic institutions to advocate for privacy rights. Engage in dialogues with policymakers, technology companies, and regulatory bodies to influence privacy-related discussions and decisions.

8. **Empowering Individuals:** Advocate for individuals' rights to access, control, and protect their personal information. Support efforts to educate individuals on privacy tools, such as virtual private networks (VPNs), encrypted messaging apps, and browser privacy extensions. Encourage individuals to exercise their rights, including making data access requests, managing privacy settings, and making informed choices about the services they use.

9. **Promoting Privacy Accountability:** Advocate for corporate accountability and responsible data practices. Encourage organizations to implement privacy governance frameworks, appoint privacy officers, and conduct regular privacy audits and assessments. Push for transparency in data collection, use, and sharing practices, and promote the adoption of robust security measures to protect personal information. Advocate for organizations to prioritize user consent, data minimization, and purpose limitation in their data handling practices.

10. **International Cooperation:** Recognize the global nature of privacy concerns and advocate for

international cooperation in privacy protection. Encourage governments, regulatory bodies, and organizations to collaborate on developing common privacy frameworks, standards, and guidelines. Support efforts to establish cross-border data transfer mechanisms that ensure consistent privacy protections when personal data flows across jurisdictions. Advocate for coordinated actions against privacy violations, cybercrime, and cross-border surveillance.

11. **Ethical Use of Data:** Promote ethical use of personal data by advocating for responsible data practices. Encourage organizations to obtain informed consent, use data for specified purposes only, and minimize data collection to what is necessary. Advocate for organizations to adopt ethical data analytics practices that respect individual privacy and avoid discriminatory profiling. Promote the development and adoption of ethical frameworks and guidelines that govern the use of data in research, AI algorithms, and emerging technologies.

12. **Public-Private Partnerships:** Advocate for collaboration between governments, private sector entities, and civil society organizations to address privacy challenges collectively. Encourage the sharing of best practices, expertise, and resources to strengthen privacy protections. Support initiatives that promote privacy-enhancing technologies, privacy research, and the development of privacy-preserving solutions. Foster dialogue and cooperation among stakeholders to develop comprehensive approaches to privacy protection.

13. **Legislative Advocacy:** Engage in legislative advocacy to influence privacy-related policies and regulations. Stay informed about proposed privacy laws and regulations and provide input through public consultations, submissions, and engagement with policymakers. Collaborate with lawmakers and advocacy groups to shape privacy legislation that reflects the evolving digital landscape and addresses emerging privacy challenges.

14. **Public Dialogue and Media Engagement:** Engage in public dialogue about privacy concerns and

promote discussions around the importance of privacy protection. Utilize media platforms to raise awareness, share knowledge, and advocate for stronger privacy protections. Publish articles, op-eds, and blog posts to educate the public about privacy rights, risks, and best practices. Participate in conferences, seminars, and public events to promote privacy awareness and engagement.

15. **Empowering Privacy Professionals:** Support the development and professional growth of privacy professionals who play a crucial role in advocating for privacy protections. Promote the recognition of privacy certifications, professional associations, and networking opportunities for privacy professionals. Encourage the continuous learning and skill development of privacy professionals to stay abreast of evolving privacy issues and emerging technologies.

Advocating for stronger privacy protections requires a multifaceted approach, combining education, policy advocacy, collaboration, and public awareness. By actively engaging in these efforts, individuals, organizations, and advocacy groups can work towards creating a privacy-respecting digital ecosystem, empowering individuals with control over their personal information, and fostering a culture that values and protects privacy rights.

Summary

Privacy in the digital age is a critical issue that requires individuals and organizations to be proactive in protecting their personal information. With the constant collection, storage, and sharing of data, it is important to understand the risks and take steps to maintain privacy. This includes being aware of privacy policies, securing devices and networks, controlling online presence, understanding data sharing practices, and advocating for stronger privacy protections.

Action Points

1. **Educate Yourself:** Start by educating yourself about the privacy landscape in the digital age. Stay

informed about data collection practices, privacy policies, and legal regulations. Understand the risks and implications of sharing personal information online, as well as the rights and protections available to you. Knowledge is the first step in taking control of your privacy.

2. **Secure Your Devices and Networks:** Implement robust security measures to protect your devices and networks. Use strong and unique passwords, enable two-factor authentication, keep software and operating systems up to date, and use encryption where possible. Secure your home Wi-Fi network and be cautious when connecting to public Wi-Fi networks. Taking these precautions helps safeguard your personal information from unauthorized access.

3. **Control Your Online Presence:** Be mindful of the information you share online and the privacy settings of your social media accounts and other online platforms. Limit the amount of personal information you disclose, review and adjust your privacy settings regularly, and be selective about accepting friend requests or connecting with unfamiliar individuals.

Think twice before posting or sharing sensitive information that could compromise your privacy.

4. **Understand Data Sharing Practices:** Be aware of how your data is collected, used, and shared by websites, apps, and online services. Read privacy policies and terms of service to understand what information is being collected, who has access to it, and how it is being used. Consider using privacy-friendly alternatives or adjusting privacy settings to minimize data sharing.

5. **Advocate for Stronger Privacy Protections:** Take an active role in advocating for stronger privacy protections. Support organizations and initiatives that promote privacy rights, engage in discussions about privacy concerns with policymakers, and stay informed about proposed privacy legislation. By being proactive and raising awareness, you contribute to the larger effort of shaping privacy regulations and promoting responsible data practices.

Chapter 7

Summary of the Book's Key Insights and Takeaways

"Cybersecurity Study Guide: Mastering Cyber Security Defense to Shield Against Identity Theft, Data breaches, Hackers, and more in the Modern Age" is a comprehensive book that provides valuable insights and practical guidance on navigating the complex landscape of cybersecurity. It equips individuals, businesses, and organizations with the knowledge and tools needed to protect themselves from cyber threats.

The book begins by establishing a foundation of understanding about cybersecurity. It explains the various types of cyber threats, such as malware, phishing, and social engineering, and highlights the importance of cybersecurity in today's interconnected world. By emphasizing the significance of adopting a cybersecurity mindset, the author encourages individuals to prioritize cybersecurity as an ongoing practice rather than an afterthought.

One of the key takeaways from the book is the importance of conducting a thorough risk assessment. Readers are guided through the process of identifying vulnerabilities, understanding potential consequences, and developing risk mitigation strategies tailored to their specific needs. This helps individuals and organizations to proactively address potential threats and protect their valuable assets.

The book also provides practical advice on securing personal devices such as smartphones, laptops, and tablets. It covers topics like strong passwords, software updates, antivirus software, and encryption to protect against unauthorized access and data breaches. By following these recommendations, readers can enhance the security of their devices and reduce the risk of cyberattacks.

Safe internet practices are another crucial aspect addressed in the book. It educates readers about the risks associated with unsafe browsing habits, downloading suspicious files, and sharing personal information online. It emphasizes the importance of using secure networks, practicing safe social media usage, and being cautious with email communications. By adopting these practices, individuals can protect their online identity and reduce the likelihood of falling victim to cyber threats.

Data protection is a central theme discussed in the book. The author highlights the significance of protecting personal and sensitive data. It explains the concept of data privacy, the risks of data breaches, and the importance of data encryption and secure backups. By implementing robust data protection measures, individuals and organizations can safeguard their information and mitigate the potential damage caused by data breaches.

Overall, *"Cybersecurity Study Guide: Mastering Cyber Security Defense to Shield Against Identity Theft, Data breaches, Hackers, and more in the Modern Age"* provides a comprehensive and practical approach to cybersecurity. It empowers readers with the knowledge and tools necessary to navigate the digital landscape securely. By adopting the insights and implementing the recommended strategies, individuals and organizations can enhance their cybersecurity posture and protect themselves from the ever-evolving cyber threats of the modern world.

Reiteration of the Importance of Cybersecurity in the Modern World

In the modern world, where digital technologies are deeply integrated into our daily lives, the importance of cybersecurity cannot be overstated. Cybersecurity is no longer just a concern for IT professionals or large organizations; it has become a critical aspect of our personal and professional lives. Here, we reiterate the significance of cybersecurity in the modern world and highlight the reasons why it should be a top priority for individuals, businesses, and governments.

First and foremost, cybersecurity is essential for protecting sensitive information and preserving privacy. In an era where personal data is collected, stored, and shared extensively, individuals are at risk of falling victim to identity theft, financial fraud, and other forms of cybercrime. By implementing robust cybersecurity measures, such as strong passwords, encryption, and secure browsing habits, individuals can safeguard their personal information and maintain control over their online identities.

Businesses and organizations face significant threats in the digital age. Cyberattacks can disrupt operations, compromise customer data, and damage reputation. The repercussions of a successful cyberattack can be severe, leading to financial losses, legal liabilities, and a loss of customer trust. By prioritizing cybersecurity, organizations can protect their valuable assets, ensure business continuity, and foster a trusted relationship with their stakeholders.

In addition to protecting personal and organizational interests, cybersecurity plays a crucial role in safeguarding national security and critical infrastructure. Governments and nations are increasingly targeted by state-sponsored cyber espionage and cyber warfare. Cyberattacks on critical infrastructure, such as power grids, transportation systems, and healthcare facilities, can have catastrophic consequences. By investing in robust cybersecurity capabilities, governments can defend against these threats and ensure the stability and security of their nations.

The evolving technological landscape brings both

opportunities and challenges. Emerging technologies like *artificial intelligence, internet of things (IoT), and cloud computing* offer immense potential, but they also introduce new vulnerabilities. Cybersecurity is essential for harnessing the benefits of these technologies while mitigating the associated risks. It enables organizations and individuals to embrace technological advancements confidently, knowing that their digital assets and privacy are adequately protected.

Another critical aspect of cybersecurity is its role in fostering trust and confidence in the digital ecosystem. When individuals and businesses have confidence in the security of their online interactions, they are more likely to engage in digital activities, such as e-commerce, online banking, and sharing sensitive information. By establishing robust cybersecurity practices and frameworks, we can build a digital environment that promotes trust, collaboration, and responsible technology use.

Furthermore, cybersecurity is an ongoing process rather than a one-time solution. It requires continuous monitoring, adaptation, and education. Cyber threats are constantly evolving, with attackers finding new ways to exploit vulnerabilities. Therefore, individuals, businesses, and governments must stay vigilant, keep up with the latest cybersecurity practices, and invest in regular training and awareness programs.

The importance of cybersecurity in the modern world cannot be overstated. It is crucial for protecting personal information, preserving privacy, ensuring business continuity, safeguarding national security, adapting to technological advancements, and fostering trust in the digital ecosystem. By prioritizing cybersecurity and adopting proactive measures, we can navigate the digital landscape safely, mitigate cyber risks, and fully embrace the benefits of the interconnected world we live in.

Encouragement for Readers to Take Action and Implement Cybersecurity Best Practices

Taking action and implementing cybersecurity best practices is crucial in today's digital landscape. The ever-increasing sophistication of cyber threats requires individuals, businesses, and governments to be proactive in protecting themselves and their valuable assets.

Here, we provide encouragement for readers to take action and embrace cybersecurity best practices to safeguard their digital lives.

1. **Recognize the importance:** The first step in taking action is understanding the significance of cybersecurity. Recognize that cyber threats are real and can have severe consequences. By acknowledging the potential risks, you empower yourself to take the necessary steps to protect your personal information, privacy, and digital assets.

2. **Stay informed:** Cybersecurity is a constantly evolving field, with new threats and vulnerabilities emerging regularly. Stay informed about the latest trends, attack techniques, and cybersecurity best practices. Follow reputable sources, attend webinars or workshops, and engage with the cybersecurity community to enhance your knowledge and awareness.

3. **Assess your current security posture:** Conduct a thorough assessment of your current security practices and identify any vulnerabilities or areas for improvement. This may include evaluating your passwords, updating software and devices, reviewing privacy settings on social media platforms, and conducting security audits of your home or office network.

4. **Implement strong passwords and multi-factor authentication:** Use unique and complex passwords for all your accounts and avoid using easily guessable information. Consider implementing multi-factor authentication, which provides an additional layer of security by requiring a second form of verification, such as a code sent to your mobile device.

5. **Keep software and devices updated:** Regularly update your operating systems, applications, and security software to ensure you have the latest security patches and protection against known vulnerabilities. Enable automatic updates whenever possible to stay protected against emerging threats.

6. **Practice safe browsing habits:** Be cautious when clicking on links, downloading attachments, or visiting unfamiliar websites. Exercise caution with email attachments, as they may contain malware. Verify the authenticity of websites before entering sensitive information and use secure HTTPS connections whenever possible.

7. **Secure your home network:** Change the default password on your home router and enable encryption (WPA2 or WPA3) to secure your Wi-Fi network. Disable remote management and regularly update your router's firmware to patch security vulnerabilities.

8. **Backup your data:** Regularly back up your important files and data to an external hard drive, cloud storage, or another secure location. This ensures that even if your system is compromised or data is lost, you can restore it from a backup.

9. **Educate yourself and others:** Educate yourself and your family, friends, or colleagues about cybersecurity best practices. Share knowledge, tips,

and resources to create a culture of cybersecurity awareness. Encourage others to be vigilant and adopt secure practices in their digital lives.

10. **Seek professional assistance if needed:** If you are uncertain about implementing cybersecurity measures or need assistance in securing your digital environment, consider seeking help from cybersecurity professionals or experts. They can provide guidance, conduct security assessments, and help you develop a robust cybersecurity strategy tailored to your specific needs.

Remember, cybersecurity is a shared responsibility. By taking action and implementing cybersecurity best practices, you not only protect yourself but also contribute to a safer digital ecosystem for everyone. Embrace the mindset that cybersecurity is an ongoing effort and commit to continuously improving your security measures. Your proactive approach to cybersecurity will help safeguard your digital life, protect your privacy, and mitigate the risks of cyber threats.

SPECIAL BONUS!

Want These 2 Bonus EBooks For Free?

Get FREE, Unlimited Access To These and All of Our New Books By Joining Our Community

CLICK HERE TO JOIN

Thank You!

Thank you for taking the time to check out my work - I hope you enjoy reading it as much as I enjoyed writing it! Authors wouldn't be anywhere without readers like you, so your support **REALLY** means a lot. I'm a firm believer that books don't need to be expensive or difficult to get hold of - so I want to encourage **EVERYONE** to enjoy the pleasure of books - and not just mine.

<u>I would be grateful if you could **WRITE ME A REVIEW** on the product detail page about how this book has helped you. Your review means a lot to me, as I would love to hear about your successes.</u>

Nothing makes me happier than knowing that my work has aided someone in achieving their goals and progressing in life; which would likewise motivate me to improve and serve you better, and also encourage other readers to get influenced positively by my work.

<u>Your feedback means so much to me, and I will never take it for granted.</u>

I'd love to hear from you if you have any recommendations

SPECIAL BONUS!

Want These 2 Bonus EBooks For Free?

Get FREE, Unlimited Access To These and All of Our New Books By Joining Our Community

CLICK HERE TO JOIN

Thank You!

Thank you for taking the time to check out my work - I hope you enjoy reading it as much as I enjoyed writing it! Authors wouldn't be anywhere without readers like you, so your support **REALLY** means a lot. I'm a firm believer that books don't need to be expensive or difficult to get hold of - so I want to encourage **EVERYONE** to enjoy the pleasure of books - and not just mine.

I would be grateful if you could **WRITE ME A REVIEW** on the product detail page about how this book has helped you. Your review means a lot to me, as I would love to hear about your successes.

Nothing makes me happier than knowing that my work has aided someone in achieving their goals and progressing in life; which would likewise motivate me to improve and serve you better, and also encourage other readers to get influenced positively by my work.

Your feedback means so much to me, and I will never take it for granted.

I'd love to hear from you if you have any recommendations

of your own, so please do get in touch if you've read anything awesome lately.

If you ever have any questions, you can get in touch at sam@samamoo.com.

I want you to enjoy your reading experience; your satisfaction is my number one priority. You are well appreciated for reading this book.

Thank you, have a wonderful day!

About The Author

I am a dynamic entrepreneur, visionary founder, and accomplished author with a passion for empowering individuals and businesses to achieve unparalleled success. With a proven track record of leadership and innovation, I have established myself as a prominent figure in the realms of entrepreneurship, publishing, and business coaching.

My professional journey has been defined by a relentless pursuit of excellence and a steadfast commitment to delivering tangible results. I take great pride in my ability to seamlessly blend strategic planning, meticulous coordination, and adept implementation of best practices to orchestrate transformative protocols and methodologies. This proficiency has consistently led to noteworthy advancements in both quality and operational processes, catalyzing organizations toward the realization of their overarching objectives.

One of my distinguishing strengths lies in my strategic acumen, which has enabled me to navigate through market shifts and anticipate emerging trends and technologies. I have a knack for identifying opportunities and harnessing innovation to enrich enterprises with substantial value. Furthermore, my reputation as a prolific content creator and publisher is underscored by my authorship of impactful books and articles spanning business, personal development, and technology. My writing prowess shines through in my ability to concisely convey intricate concepts, making them accessible to diverse audiences.

Connect with me here:

Instagram: https://instagram.com/_amoosam

Facebook: https://fb.me/samamoo.official

Twitter: https://twitter.com/samamooofficial

LinkedIn: https://www.linkedin.com/company/samamoo

Email: sam@samamoo.com

Website: https://samamoo.com

Other Books

- How to be More in Tune with The Feelings of Your Customers
- Time Management For Busy People

- Sell Like titans

www.ingramcontent.com/pod-product-compliance
Lightning Source LLC
LaVergne TN
LVHW051225050326
832903LV00028B/2252